ENDORSEMENTS

"In Courting With Chance, Karen Gauff courageously relays a vivid memoir of her life's journey in the most interesting reflections that carries the reader from beginning to end."

David Chaney, Esq., Adjunct Professor, Chief Asst. Attorney General (Ret.)

"Courting With Chance is a Must Read for ALL! This memoir is truly an intense yet inspirational tell all life portrait. Karen is unyieldingly transparent in sharing her gritty and moving journey which teaches how to overcome defeat, peril and low self-esteem through education, spiritual nurturing, forgiveness, and ultimate trust in the saving power of the name of Jesus. Simply Triumphant!"

Sara Alford-McIntosh MD, Dual Board-Certified American Board of Psychiatry and Neurology, American Board of Addiction Medicine

This book is dedicated to all those who poured into

my life.

Sanari,
Thank you for supporting my
life - assignment.
Remember, nothing happens by
chance when you rock with
Jesus!
                    Love
                Kay Hartt
                        10/9/23

Courting with Chance
Reconciling Memoirs

by

Karen A. Gauff

MY INSPIRATION

Courage allows the successful woman to fail –
And to learn powerful lessons from the failure –
So that in the end, she didn't fail at all.

Maya Angelou

PREFACE

I considered writing my autobiography near the end of my legal career, but, in 2009, everything changed when I found a ninety-six-page typed manuscript written by my mother. It was entitled, "The Plight of a Welfare Mother."

My mother said she wrote the manuscript as her explanation to her six living children regarding the period of a little over a year when she was in a mental institution and for the darkness that plagued her mind on her painful journey back to sanity. Mom's story, by her own admission, is a vivid illustration of how the cunningness and deceitfulness of two adults, Mom and Dad, negatively impacted the lives of others, and almost ruined the lives of their children.

Thus, my story, "Courting with Chance," is about the likelihood I would have had a successful life at all given I was born the eighth child to parents experiencing domestic violence crisis, insanity and poverty that nearly exploded our family. Courting with Chance is a reconciliation of my mother's perspective and my own, along with my revelation of why I was given a chance to miraculously transform the insanity, pain and ugliness that shaped my life into life-affirming possibilities resulting in me sitting as a Judge.

THANK YOU

Thank you, Mom for giving me a chance to live and for taking the time to leave a written explanation for so many of my questions. Thank you, Dad for reaching out, when you could. Thank you, Deila for doing your best. Thank you, Paulette for giving me a chance to see Christ. Thank you, Granny and Papa Curry for giving me a safe, happy and peaceful home. Thank you, Claudia for inspiring me, teaching me and loving me like your own. Thank you, my son, Brandon, for reminding me that I am just Mom. Thank you, my son, Marshawno, for accepting me as your Mom. Thank you to my husband, Will, for being so understanding while I searched within. Thank you to my advance team: Sharon, Cherlyn and Suparna, for helping me document my story and for your insightfulness. Thank you to the Los Angeles Superior Court for protecting me as a child and giving me a chance to protect others as a judge. Thank you to all those angels along the way who encouraged me to write a book about my journey.

SPECIAL ACKNOWLEDGEMENT

Karen Earls Flores, Esq., I am forever indebted for your kindness in embracing me as the other side of your brain and for editing my story. I so appreciate all the fights we had to get this project to the finish line. You are the best of the best!

DISCLAIMER

Please note, this memoir is a compilation of my mother's recollections of events, as discovered in her manuscript, and my recollection of events, experiences and perceptions since my birth. I have related them to the best of my knowledge. Some identities have been changed.

Author Photographs by Cherlyn J. Clark

of Crimson Photography

Book Design by Rae Design Studio

CONTENTS

CONTENTS

COURTING WITH CHANCE
Reconciling Memoirs

CHAPTER 1

What Are The Chances Of That?

Sometimes life experiences and situations seem to occur randomly to the naked eye. Looking back over the past fifty years of my life, I can tell you with certainty that nothing is as simple as it seems to the naked eye. Simply stated, nothing is by chance.

In my present judicial assignment, I preside over a misdemeanor and drug court calendar. My cases often involve family restoration issues in one form or another. Sometimes I see pain in the eyes of the victims and defendants that I encounter daily. At times I wonder if there is shame lurking underneath the pain. I also recognize that I could have easily been any one of those victims or defendants. In this memoir, I am starting the conversation of exposing shame beneath the pain to help others recognize their own power and strength of overcoming, surviving and even triumphing over seemingly unfathomable life experiences.

I am hopeful that as you read my memoir you will keep in mind that my story is still unfolding. Although I started the journey of sharing this memoir many years ago, it was the year before my judicial appointment that I gained the insight of how to put my story into print with a little help from my mother.

After appearing in court and conducting two client conference calls earlier in the day in the spring of 2009, it slipped my mind that I had promised my newly hired insurance consultant, Joseph, that I would bring him my existing insurance policies for our meeting the next day in Sacramento, California. Initially, I avoided Joseph's phone calls like the plague because I figured he was just another insurance salesman that I didn't have time, energy or a need for. I thought I had enough life, disability and gap insurance for me and my son, Brandon. I only accepted Joseph's call because he told me that he was referred to me by my mother, Pearl Ackerson.

Joseph knew how to start the conversation by pulling my emotional strings in our first phone call. He said, "When I met your mother, Mrs. Ackerson, she talked about you nonstop. She couldn't stop talking about her daughter, the attorney, who lived in Los Angeles. She told me that she couldn't afford our product, but she wanted me to make sure that I spoke with you. She is so proud of you."

At first, I was caught off guard because of Joseph's use of the "mother" card. But I knew he didn't know that Ms. Pearl, my Dad's widow, was my stepmother, not my mother. I also didn't want to explain the long-sorted details of my relationship with Ms. Pearl.

When I was a child, I tolerated Ms. Pearl because I only knew her through the eyes of my mother and the few summer interactions, I saw of her while visiting my Dad after my parent's divorced. As an adult, I learned to respect and honor Ms. Pearl because I realized the many sacrifices, she made in merging her family with ours.

By 2009, because both of my natural parents were deceased, Ms. Pearl was the only remaining parent figure alive in Sacramento. She held portions of my parent's secrets because she was the other woman during their marriage. I continued to visit Ms. Pearl whenever I traveled to Sacramento for work or otherwise.

I didn't want to disappoint her, so I agreed to meet with Joseph. I met him and was pleasantly surprised that he might have a product that could benefit me. After sharing that I wanted to do business with Joseph, he asked me to bring my insurance portfolio to our next scheduled meeting.

Once I arrived back home to Los Angeles, I dreaded looking for my existing insurance policies mostly because I hated clutter, yet I knew that my important papers were packed away in boxes that held all the clutter in my world. I managed to get my energy level up to pull the black box from the bottom of my master bathroom's linen closet. I rifled through it and pulled out a couple of insurance policies. I was relieved that they were easier to put my hands on than I thought. Just as I was returning the extra papers to the box, I saw my Mom's driver's license fall from between the papers. I picked up the license, looked at it and noted just how much I favored her, which I had heard all my life. After taking just a fleeting moment to reflect, I looked down at the extra papers on my lap and saw a typed document with editing marks on it, peaking out of the pile. It read, "The Plight of a Welfare Mom." As I picked up the document and started browsing through it, I realized I was holding a buried family treasure. I sat in awe first feeling as if I was reading my Mom's diary. It was a type written ninety-six paged, double-spaced manuscript drafted by my mother.

But for Ms. Pearl sending the insurance salesman my way to look for my insurance policies, I probably would have never run across this manuscript. The fact that Ms. Pearl, my Dad's second wife and my Mom's nemesis was somehow involved in me finding Mom's manuscript, was ironic to say the least. What are the chances of that?

CHAPTER 2

Mom's Chance To Succeed

Finding Mom's ninety-six-page manuscript about her life put so many things in perspective for me in relation to my family's history and answers to all my lifelong questions. Let me begin by sharing Mom's perspective from her manuscript:

Mom was born Mable Lily in 1934 in Bakersfield, California, to Pinkey and Elnora Lily. Mom was the third oldest of seven children. Her siblings were Cecil, Betty, Bob, Gus, Henrietta and Pinkey. Mom was a great listener as a child, because in her generation children were supposed to be seen and not heard. Mom said, when she was a little girl, she sat and listened to her parents talk about the difficult days of the Great Depression and how during those times very few black men were able to get jobs. She overheard them say because of the droughts, Mom's grandfathers on both

sides, her father, uncles and aunts, bundled up all the family in Oklahoma and migrated to California's San Joaquin Valley and settled in Bakersfield in the early 1930s. Mom's family was a part of The Dust Bowl Migration which forced tens of thousands of families to abandon their farms in Oklahoma and move to California because of a period of severe dust storms.

Mom said her Dad was tall with mahogany smooth skin, weighing approximately 250 lbs. He was referred to as a lawyer because he was so smart, and he had an unusual sort of round head. Also, he had a mouth full of gold which made him look handsome with his unblemished deep skin. He didn't like working for others, so he turned to farming and contracting.

Mom described her mother as a brown skinned woman standing 5'4, wearing a size five shoe, and weighing about 140 lbs. until she got the middle age spread. Mom viewed her mother as very humble and she always appeared to be afraid of Mom's father.

Mom also remembered thinking her father always yelled and cursed when talking to her mother. He would leave for three or more days and return raving, kicking open the front door and slinging things out of the way. All the kids would run to their mother to try to protect her. They decided, if their Dad was going to fight her, he had to first get them out of the way.

Mom also shared that she didn't remember her

mother never going grocery or clothes shopping like most mothers did. She always sent Mom or one of her siblings with a note for groceries. If it was a small item they needed, like hamburger meat, and the children could not be found, her mother would send the family dog, Brownie, to the store with a note in his mouth. Brownie had been taught how to open the store door with his paws, deliver the note, and return home with the food items around his neck.

Mom explained she saw a lifeless change in her mother for some time. Mom noticed that all of sudden her mother stopped going outside. It was as if she was afraid of leaving out the front door. Mom said her mother seemed like she was in a depressed state or syndrome. She lost interest in preparing meals for her children and became involved with Voo-Doo. Mom noticed her mother grew accustomed to sitting in the dark with the shades down. She also started a collection of candles, including one as tall as a quart jar and two inches wide and one white candle about three inches wide with a black cat on it with its tail sticking straight in the air, as if it was angry.

As Mom listened to visitors in the house, she noticed her mother was regarded as a counselor. People came to her who were plagued with ailments like lunacy, loss of loved ones, illnesses and were going through divorces. Mom also thought the families' money was spent on candles and powders because of Voo-Doo. Mom said a wedge of resentment formed between her parents. Soon after, Mom's father divorced her mother and married Mrs. Mary in 1944.

After the divorce, Mom's mother was hospitalized on several occasions at Modesto State Hospital for nervous breakdowns. Mom's father drove her and her siblings to Bakersfield only once to see their mother before her hospitalization. Mom said she sensed her mother talked off during those visits, but Mom didn't understand the full impact of her mother's condition. Mom said she did have sense enough to know from past experience with her mother, along with her past governing inadequacies, her mother's nervous condition rendered her incapable of managing or handling a family.

Mom was the namesake to her maternal aunt, Mable. Mom's mother looked up to Aunt Mable. Aunt Mable lived in Berkeley, California, and whenever she came to San Joaquin Valley, she always looked immaculate and drove a new car. She worked hard and always spent time and money on Mom and her siblings. Aunt Mable was one of the few people Mom's mother would open up to. Mom thought, if anyone knew her mother's condition, Aunt Mable knew it because she visited the state hospital and talked with the doctors. Knowing Aunt Mable as Mom did, she figured Aunt Mable was hoping for a miracle and maybe she hoped her sister would just snap out of the mental illness.

Although Mom and her siblings continued to live

with her father and stepmother, Mom couldn't help but worry about her mother's condition, even after her mother was released from the hospital. Mom said, to relieve stress, she started going to church and became a part of a singing group which traveled locally. When something very satisfying happened to Mom, she got "happy." One time, Mom said she was singing, "The Lord Will Make a Way Somehow," when she opened her mouth and the Lord Jesus took over. Unaware she left the other girls on stage, without a microphone, and Mom walked down the church isle singing her song.

In addition to church, Mom also kept herself distracted from her mother's condition by writing speeches. Mom shared she was a good writer who entered and won second place in a speech contest. The night she won $50, she visited her mother and her mother's new husband, James Samuel Gordon, Jr.

Around this same time, Mom met Ann Kurt in 1950. Mom said Ann was an only child who had been placed in foster care because her mother died, and her father was too old to care for her. She lived a far distance from their school, Bakersfield High. Ann didn't have transportation to get to school functions, so it made her vulnerable to the young men on campus. She got into a lot of trouble with the boys because she appeared to be easy. Boys took advantage of her because she lived so far out. Mom told her, "I'd go to the police rather than let boys use me." No one was interested or asked questions about how Ann got

oldest sister, Betty, married and moved away. Mrs. Mary was doing the best she could to try to care for Mom, Bob, Gus, Henrietta and Pinkey, but times were hard. After the principal explained the rules, Mom complied and made sure she did not miss any more graduation practice exercises.

While finishing up high school, Mom worked for a middle-aged Jewish lady. Fortunately, it was close to Mom's school. Mom could walk there after taking the school bus. The house was huge for a three-bedroom home. Mom was awestruck by the six French windows in the living room and French windows throughout the house. The kitchen floor was white at one time but appeared to be dirty grey because it was so filthy. Mom polished the mahogany furniture throughout to perfection and worked hard to please. Mom cleaned the house top to bottom on her hands and knees. So, it was a low blow at the end of her eight hours when the woman didn't want to pay Mom the minimum wage, which was $1.25 an hour. Because Mom was so young, the woman wanted to know who Mom had worked for who paid her that kind of money. Mom named several people. Finally, Mom grew tired of arguing and told the woman, "If you don't pay me, I'll call the police." That's the only way Mom got her money. Mom never returned.

Mom then went to her school counselor and told her about how there was never any dinner for Mom when she got home from school. The counselor got Mom some work with a teacher who had two small children

Mom worked as a mother's helper.

Mom's high school graduation was the happiest day in her life up to that point. After graduation, Mom went to work for a company about fifty miles outside of Bakersfield in Mojave, California. The company was managed by a thirty-five-year old Texan, Donnie Cracker. Mom said Donnie was talkative, and would have his little say, then move fast to get out of the way before the timber fell. He was dark brown skinned and medium build with a devilish smirk on his face as he always talked about sex. He appeared to be bright until he started talking about his women, then one would realize he was a pushover. Mom said Donnie went on and on about the money he threw around for sex and how much he enjoyed making love. He told Mom, "I just love to screw." Then he would go back to the time when he was first married. Right away Mom wanted to meet his wife and family. Mom felt she had to do that to make him, the wolf, respect her and to keep him at a distance.

Mom said it all amounted to sexual harassment which was highly ignored in the fifties. Mom was on the defense and had no choice. She needed to work. If she had to run in order to get out of the way and keep her job, she did what she had to do.

Donnie tried every way conceivable to get Mom in bed with him. Mom told him point blank, "I never had sex and I'm saving myself for marriage." At that point, he raved on saying, "the man who will finally get you…" Mom slept in her pants at night because she had to share the same trailer with Donnie. He was bold and had other women and didn't care who knew it.

Finally, a couple of weeks later, Mom met Donnie's wife. She was light brown skinned, a little taller than her husband with shoulder length hair. She wasn't pretty or ugly. Right away, she reminded Mom of her own mother. She was so meek that she didn't demand anything, not even a decent place to live. The family lived in an old box car which had been converted into living quarters with two shanty make-believe bedrooms. There was so much self-denial and hurt in Mrs. Cracker's face, she could barely look Mom in the face when they talked.

Mom said Mrs. Cracker seemed overwhelmed with their four children, including two with Down syndrome. She could hardly hold a conversation because the children constantly demanded attention. Mom said she felt sad for this wife and mother who seemed to have the weight of the world on her shoulders and a jerk for a husband.

CHAPTER 3

Taking A Chance On Love

Mom said she was out of high school for two years, depressed, hurt and bewildered when she met my Dad, Allen Ackerson, a twenty-year-old native of Okmulgee, Oklahoma. Dad's father's name was Clarence Nelson and his mother was Orelia Simon. However, Dad's mother was married to another man, Tad Ackerson, at the time Dad was conceived. Dad was given his stepfather's last name, Ackerson, to keep down the neighborhood gossip. Dad was also the middle son between Vincent Ackerson and Roy Simms. Dad entered the United States (U.S.) Army in 1950 and rose to the rank of Sergeant. He served in the Korean War.

Up until meeting Dad, Mom said she hadn't allowed herself to think of love or marriage. She had a depressing image of marriage in her mind because of her parent's relationship.

Courting with Chance

Mom said she actually met Dad while she was out on a date with Sgt. Barry Juicer. When Barry picked Mom up for a dance at Roscoe Gordon's, Sgt. Ackerson was in the car. After being introduced to Sgt. Ackerson, Mom thought it was the end of it. She actually suggested they pick up her high school friend, Pam Ants, to hang out with Sgt. Ackerson, but Pam was unsure of herself and showed it. She looked like she was scared all the time and dragged her feet as she walked. While chatting with Sgt. Ackerson, Mom discovered he had previously dated her high school friend, Ann Kurt. Once they got to the dance, everyone went different directions. Mom's date was a drinker, so he headed to the bar. The place was so crowded you rarely bumped into anyone you knew. Mom actually doesn't know how Sgt. Ackerson found her because she thought he was shy. He looked bashful with beautiful light brown skin though he had ringworms all over his face. He was 5'9 weighed 185 lbs. He looked like a model with the exception of the ringworms.

Mom felt someone pecking on her shoulder. She turned around; it was Sgt. Ackerson. He majestically led her to the center of the dance floor. Once they danced, she couldn't shake him, and he wouldn't let go. Everywhere Mom went, he held her hand. He'd sing to her, "You may not know you're an angel, you may not know that I care, oh my darling you're an angel and I'll always be in love with you," by Johnnie Ace.

That was the first and last time anything like that ever happened to Mom. Mom use to close her eyes and she would visualize Dad singing to her. That night was the beginning of many beautiful nights and days together. Mom called Dad, Ale, for short. She said Ale liked soul food, so when he came to town from Camp Richards, he grabbed Mom and they headed for Mom's Café, which was one of the best soul food kitchens on Cottonwood Road in Bakersfield. There, they ate from the same plate. Mom didn't have much of an appetite, just seeing Dad seemed to fill her up.

Mom said she loved the fact Dad was an eternal jokester. He never met a situation he couldn't laugh at. He also had very thick skin because he could take a joke as well as give one.

When near Dad, Mom said her adrenalin gland functioned overtime which seemed to make her heartbeat irregularly. Mom was sexless, but, yet sensuous to his touch and found it hard to keep her sensitivity under control. Mom never felt that close to anyone before. She felt she had everything and her physical attraction to Dad was hard to overlook or deny.

Mom confessed she was pregnant when she and Dad were married on January 5, 1954, by a judge with only Mom's mother and sister, Betty, in attendance. Dad had just turned twenty-one and received his honorable discharge from the Army.

Courting with Chance

Just two months later, my oldest brother, Allen Jr. nicknamed Bull, was born in Bakersfield. Dad was thrilled because Bull was his first son and a spitting image of Dad. Shortly thereafter, Mom and Dad moved to Corcoran, California. They were so immature. They didn't stop to think jobs were limited in a small town. Dad tried irrigating, but he was no good at it. He had never done farm labor before, so he found it difficult. Next, he tried bucking hay. After a day of it, he didn't want to eat, just sleep.

Bull was almost two years old when Dad's Mom, Orelia, and her newest husband, William Kennedy, visited from Okmulgee, Oklahoma. Mom described Dad's mom as short with a round face, not skinny and not fat, just in between. Mom said she was also talkative and rattled on and on about what they had back in Oklahoma and about being president of the usher board at her church. They didn't leave until Mom and Dad promised to move to Oklahoma.

Meanwhile, in November 1955 in Corcoran, Mom gave birth to my oldest sister, Beverly Ann, born at 7lbs 12 oz. Beverly was only six months old when she was hospitalized for pneumonia and the doctors discovered her enlarged heart. She never made it back home. Mom, Dad and Bull were devastated and missed Beverly terribly.

Mom said their marriage was never the same after Beverly Ann's death. It seemed to fall apart at the seams. Mom and Dad thought moving back to Bakersfield might help. So, they packed up and moved back to a suburb in Bakersfield called Carversville.

On one unforgettable Saturday morning, Dad told Mom he was going to wash his car. Mom and Bull waited until after lunch for Dad to return. Because Dad still wasn't back, Mom decided to take Bull and walk four blocks over to visit Ann Kurt, Mom's high school friend and Dad's ex-girlfriend. They visited Ann for about two hours and returned home.

Upon Mom and Bull's arrival home, Dad was waiting for them and he was angry. As soon as Mom told Dad where they had been, he gave Mom a back-hand slap with his open hand right in the center of her face, then he set her up for a repeat left and right to the face with his fist, most landing near her eyes. Mom was totally in shock and unable to defend herself. She couldn't even believe it was happening. Blood began to trickle down from a cut in her right eyebrow. Mom's eyes became swollen so fast she could barely see as she ran out of the house.

Mom left Bull and proceeded to walk the three miles to her grandparents' home while looking back all the way. Mom couldn't help but think how dangerous it was to be walking down Cottonwood Road after dark. She didn't dare want to think about her classmate who had traveled the same route and was kidnapped, raped by four men, and burnt with cigarettes before being left-for-dead on a nearby country road. Mom didn't care because she just knew she had to get away from

Dad and get to safety.

Mom made it to her grandparent's house, Grandpa and Grandma Penrice. They were seventy-five and seventy-four years old respectively. Grandpa Penrice saw Mom first. He was furious when he found out what happened. He brought Mom in and Grandma gave Mom aid while Grandpa walked two blocks to get the police. Mom had passed the police call box, but she was too embarrassed to stop.

The two policemen, one a rookie and one veteran officer, followed Grandpa back to his house. By then Mom could barely open both of her eyes. They took a report, including a description of Dad's car. Before they left, the rookie officer said to Mom, "If we can find your husband, we'll put him away and it'll be a long time before he can do this to you again."

Yet, Mom went back to Dad believing him when he told her he would never hit her again.

Mom said that beating brought a lot of things into clear focus for her. She remembered the first time Dad hurt her emotionally. Mom said when she was in her last month of pregnancy with Bull, Mom and Dad went on a double date with Mom's sister, Henrietta, and her boyfriend. They ended up staying over-night in a run-down motel in Fresno. Two prostitutes were flirting with Dad when they arrived and upon their departure. Among other things, one of the prostitutes pointed at Dad and said, "Next time, you come alone." It didn't really bother Mom until she saw how frustrated Dad became. Dad got all upset and began to twist and turn in his seat. Henrietta's date said to Dad, "what's the matter with you?" Dad leaned over the front seat and whispered something in his ear. In response, the man said, "I wouldn't tell my wife that." Dad took the dare and responded, "I want some different pussy!" Mom was so embarrassed for Dad's lack of respect. She sat numb and speechless, like her mother, all the way back home.

Mom said she didn't realize it then, but she began keeping score for the payback. She also shared the following about score keeping: "No one really wins when couples turn into scorekeepers. When scorekeeping occurs, one or both partners expect "fair reimbursement" for each action performed in their mate's behalf. If one mate gives the other a luxurious weekend away at a resort, without saying it, the other mate expects something just as elaborate in return. Couples even keep score as to how often one washes dishes. Women do this unconsciously, if both work, one night one might refuse to do dishes because one mate feels the other hasn't done his fair share. If you would like to avoid bitterness in a relationship, and if you would like to avoid emotional distress further up the road, listen to the following: One, you should never do things for your partner with strings attached. Don't expect someone to respond every time you do something for him or her. Two, don't try to pressure your partner into doing something to "even the score."

In other words, don't try to get your partner to do something he or she doesn't want to do. Three, never do something to "even the score" yourself. When you do, your relationship seems more like a business arrangement than true love. In the ultimate end, score cards don't work. If you don't want to involve yourselves in a power struggle, keep away from score-keeping."

CHAPTER 4

Crazy Chance

Mom and Dad decided to keep their word to Grandma Orelia and move to Oklahoma. Mom said she was conflicted because she believed Dad had been involved with several women but thought a move to Oklahoma was best to get those women out of his system. She thought it would solve that problem. They were in Oklahoma only a short time before Mom was shocked into reality and her dreams were shattered by all the dysfunction in Dad's family, too.

First, Mom realized Dad's mother was an alcoholic. And in 1956, Mom thought the prohibition era was still in effect. Mom was scared stiff while in Okmulgee because when visiting friends or relatives, she had no way of knowing who sold illegal whiskey. Mom lived in fear of being arrested because of being in the wrong place at the wrong time. She just didn't want to go to jail. Dad would tell her, "Mable, you talk too much!"

Also, while there, inevitably, some relative would get drunk and start a huge fight which sometimes ended up in unbelievable violence between Dad, his younger brother, Roy, and others. Mom told of having to help Dad in a fight one time when Dad confronted Uncle Roy about stealing money. In response, Uncle Roy strong- armed Dad to the ground and commenced choking him. Mom was so afraid. She hit Uncle Roy in the head with a frying pan to keep him from choking Dad to death. Once Dad got up, he went and got his gun and fired at Uncle Roy. Mom said Grandma Orelia just cried like a baby when she witnessed this particular fight between her sons.

Then Mom discovered she was pregnant again. This time it was with my brother, Matthew, nicknamed Mutt. Over the next three years, Mom had two more children: Deila, nicknamed "Black gal," and Paulette, nicknamed "Yellow gal." They later earned other nicknames from us, their siblings; Dig and Hop, respectively.

Mom said that she found herself pregnant every one and a half years. She was starting to convince herself that Dad was always being distracted by other women. Mom thought because Dad was so good looking, he could not concentrate on being a faithful husband and father. Mom also saw Dad wasn't trying to further educate himself. Once Mom realized Dad didn't want to further his education to make things better for the family, she was never the same.

Mom's brother, Bob, had joined the U.S. Marine Corps Reserve. It wasn't long before he talked Dad into doing the same. Dad went into the Reserves as a sergeant since it was his last rank in the Army. On Dad's first two week's summer stint, his lieutenant liked his work and told him, "If you stick with me, the sky would be the limit." In observing Dad, Mom noted how much Dad missed the military and she decided he wasn't ready for civilian life. Mom thought Dad was lost in the outside world.

Mom noticed Dad talked to her in the same manner he talked to his recruits. Dad never could hold his liquor and after a few drinks, he was loaded. He would shout out orders to Mom telling her, "When I say shit, you shit, but if I say don't shit, god damn it, don't shit!"

Mom said, after enduring Dad's foul orders whenever he got drunk, she learned a valuable lesson, which is, there are some things you just don't say to your mate. Mom said, "Once you say something crude, you can never take it back, and some remarks can cut like a knife. In other words, what you say just doesn't stab on contact, the knife keeps grinding farther and farther into your heart until you get to a breaking point. And, then you snap."

Dad's deployments caused more family crisis. While Dad was away for military training, Mom had an affair and got pregnant. Mom knew she had to tell Dad the truth when he returned. She also had visions it wouldn't go over well, so she waited as long as she could. She finally got up enough nerve to tell him. Dad was angry and his ego was hurt. Dad was also feeling guilt-ridden because he knew he had secretly fathered another child while he was away on military duty, as well. Dad did not reveal his secret.

One night after Dad was drinking, he and Mom got into a huge argument. Dad became enraged and threatened to kick the baby out of Mom's stomach. Mom was angry and afraid when she yelled back, "You just go to sleep!" (In her mind, she added, "son-of- a-bitch!"). Dad did not take Mom's words as a threat because Mom had never threatened him or defended herself before. So, Dad disregarded Mom's words and went to sleep. As Dad laid sleep in a drunken stupor, Mom poured scalding hot water all over his body. Dad sustained third degree burns from his neck to his ankles. He had to learn how to walk again over the next six months.

While Dad was recovering, Mom took Bull, Mutt, Dig and Hop and moved back to California. Upon returning to California, Mom and the children headed to Fresno, where Mom gave birth to my brother, Eddie, nicknamed Bolo. Mom was overwhelmed with guilt. She suffered a nervous breakdown and was placed in a mental institution for nearly a year in Berkeley, California. While Mom was hospitalized, the children were placed into foster care.

After Dad's full recovery, he came to visit the kids at the foster home. While visiting, he asked to take them out for ice cream and, while out, Dad kidnapped all the kids and headed back to Oklahoma.

Upon arriving in Oklahoma, Dad found work, a babysitter in his mother, and a girlfriend next door. Dad and the kids appeared to be doing well for a little over a year, when Dad received a call from Mom's brother, Bob. He contacted Dad to inform him the doctors believed Mom would regain her mental stability, if she had a way of visiting with the children. Dad agreed   to allow Mom to come to Oklahoma to be with the children.

Mom arrived in Oklahoma and got off the airplane with a baby in her arms. The baby was introduced to Dad as Jason, whose father was a barber in Berkeley. Jason was nicknamed Hootnanne.

Dad tried to adjust to Mom and the surprise of Hootnanne, but after about six months, Mom was cramping Dad's style. This was extremely difficult, especially since at least one of Dad's girlfriends lived next door. Plus, Dad was still dealing with emotional scarring from being burned by Mom. Mom was also miserable and pregnant again; this time, with me. Apparently, Dad's next-door girlfriend was pregnant too. Mom came up with an exit strategy which she kept to herself. She waited until Dad left for work and the big kids went to school. Mom packed up the car, picked up the big kids, with the exception of Bolo, because Grandma Orelia was babysitting him. Dad came home to find only Bolo with Grandma Orelia.

Courting with Chance

Dad was devastated when he realized Mom took the other children and returned to California.

While still in Oklahoma, Dad and Bolo developed an unbreakable bond. Once Mom and the other kids made it back to California, they headed straight to Bakersfield this time. Mom moved into a shotgun two-bedroom, apartment down the walkway from her mother and stepfather.

Mom gave birth to me, Karen Monique, in February 1965, and nicknamed me Nikkie because of my middle name.

Dad returned to California the next year, brought Bolo to Bakersfield, met me, and then moved to Sacramento, California.

CHAPTER 5

My Chance To Live

With respect to my perspective, my first memory is of me riding my tricycle around the little set of apartments near Cottonwood Road, down the sidewalk from my grandparents without a worry in the world. My middle sister, Hop, took a special interest in me from the start. She seemed to enjoy teaching me how to ride my tricycle. I also had a lot of fuss made over me. When asked my name, Mom said my reply was, "I Nikkie." You see, Nikkie could do no wrong! Along the way, I gained another nickname, "Love," from Mom.

While I was attending preschool, Mom had help for me from her Uncle Johnnie's wife, Aunt Vern. She picked me up from preschool, took me to Der Wienerschnitzel for a hot dog daily after school, and kept me until Mom picked me up. I was in seventh heaven until one day

Courting with Chance

Mom and Aunt Vern had an argument. Sadly, I never went to Aunt Vern's after school again.

About one year later, after becoming a tricycle pro, I peered through the kindergarten gate, I watched the big kids and was excited I would soon be joining them on the other side of the gate when I made it to the first grade. At home, I ran around playing with my two brothers: Bolo and Hootnanne. Hootnanne was my nemesis and Bolo was my protector from Hootnanne. So, when Hootnanne used me as a punching bag and gave me a black eye, for talking smart to him, Bolo decided to even the score and Hootnanne ended up with two black eyes. This was my first introduction to justice.

During these years, I viewed Mom's stepfather, Grandpa Gordon, as my father because I saw him every day unlike my Dad who only came to visit periodically. Plus, in my eyes it seemed that I had more freedoms with Grandpa Gordon around than my Dad.

I learned how to manipulate Mom early on. But I also learned the hard way that my shenanigans worked best when Dad wasn't around. One trick was me pretending I had an uncontrollable bout with the hiccups which typically resulted in Mom scrambling to buy me a 7up. On one weekend when Dad was visiting us, I started my hiccups bout, but before Mom could jump into action to get me a 7up, Dad told her not to move because he had something that would stop my hiccups. Dad pulled out a belt. I never had a problem with hiccups again.

After that, I really preferred to hang out with Grandpa Gordon than Dad because I knew I could have anything I wanted when I was with Grandpa Gordon.

Grandpa Gordon was tall with medium brown skin, salt and pepper hair, and he wore eyeglasses. He loved sitting on the front porch drinking a beer and eating a whole raw onion. He was just as happy as could be sitting there telling me stories. This seemed to be Grandpa's escape from Grandma because she just sat in the front window and stared aimlessly for hours every day. Instead of cursing when he got angry at me or others, he would say, "You awnna forgotten turkey trodden got dandruff in your head." Grandpa also loved to scare me. Sometimes when we walked down Cottonwood Road, he liked to say he was going to send me to Mr. Rucker. Mr. Rucker was the neighborhood mortician who looked very creepy. So, I was scared straight every time he mentioned Mr. Rucker.

When I was about five years old, one evening, I walked to the liquor store with Grandpa. Upon entering the store, I rushed around the corner to the candy aisle. When I turned the corner, I ran smack into a middle-aged woman who was headed to the cash register. I said, "Oh, excuse me, I'm so sorry." She responded, "Oh, ok" and gave me a look of excusing my mannish behavior and allowed me to pass. After Grandpa paid for his beer and my Hot Tamales (my favorite candy), we walked toward the door. As soon as Grandpa opened the door, we heard a loud crashing noise and a terrifying scream. At the same time, I looked toward the sound of the noise and I saw a body flying in the air and a car in front of it. Grandpa tried to grab my face and cover my eyes, but it was too late. Once everything came to a pause, I realized the lady I had just ran into inside the store, was now lying on the ground in front of me. She was moaning for a few minutes, then she stopped. People were frantic running all over the place and trying to get people to call for an ambulance. I heard someone say, "She's dead!" I did not have any idea what dead meant. But I did know it meant she would go to see Mr. Rucker. I was terrified for her.

Upon returning to my Grandparent's home, Grandpa explained to me what death meant. He said the dead women would never walk, talk, move or breathe again on earth. From then on, I thought it was my life's calling to investigate death and determine what happened to people when they died.

Mom never minded me spending time with Grandpa because I was just down the walkway from our apartment. It took a couple of years of Mom being alone with just us children for her to get her bearings. During this period, she began dating a man named Jerry. Mom was so happy in those days. She said she felt like she finally found herself.

Soon after, Mom was able to find us a house and we were happy to move away from the apartment even though I missed Grandpa. The new house carried really special memories because it was big enough for all of us. It was next to the cemetery where our oldest sister, Beverly Ann, was buried. We used to play hide and seek in the backyard. My older siblings loved scaring us with stories about the cemetery behind our house, too.

While Mom was going to school, Bull was our babysitter. This was right up his alley because he just lived up to his nickname by bossing everyone around. He literally put the others on a timer to force them to clean the house to his liking, while he set around and ate junk food my other brothers stole at Bull's direction. I wasn't really included when it came to Bull's wrath because he knew I would tell Mom everything. As a matter of fact, I picked up a new nickname, "Tape-recorder," because of my tattle- telling skills. I remembered all the graphic details and left nothing out.

It didn't help a couple of years later, when my cousin, Jacob, pushed me down to the sidewalk and scarred my face. The scar spurred my siblings on to take the teasing to a new level. With it came a new nickname, "Bump." They pretended they were pushing the button on my forehead to rewind all of the day's events. It was so humiliating, but I learned to have very thick skin because of my early experiences with teasing.

Also, during this period, the boys began getting into trouble and Mom decided she couldn't go to school or work because she was spending most of her time at juvenile court. Bull at fourteen years old, weighing 160 lbs., trained all the other kids to steal. When Mom found out the truth, she couldn't handle it and it was just about too late. Mom also realized she couldn't chastise Bull because he would grab the belt and hold Mom's hands behind her back and just look at her and smile. In addition, Bull was introduced to nude magazines he found underneath the sofa. They were left by Mom's brother, Uncle Gus, when he slept overnight. Unfortunately, this was the beginning of the incestuous behavior which would mar our entire childhood.

CHAPTER 6

A Chance For The Family To Work

I heard my older siblings saying Dad was back to get us. I was too young to realize everything going on, but I knew everybody was happy. Dad had returned to move us all to Sacramento because he and Mom were getting back together. Hooray, happy days, or so we thought.

We had two events we were excited to attend before moving to Sacramento with Dad. The first was the seventy-fifth wedding anniversary for Mom's grandparents, Grandpa and Grandma Penrice who were both nearly one hundred years old. They lived in Berkeley with Mom's Aunt Mable. The couple of memories I had of my great grandparents letting us play with their wheelchairs and watching them help one another because Grandma was blind and Grandpa was hard of hearing, were all fond memories. Mom ended up going to their celebration without us because she said she couldn't afford to take all of us kids.

The second event was our Cousin Lisa's wedding. Fortunately, it was taking place in Bakersfield the next month. Since Lisa's wedding was my first wedding, Mom warned me to be careful and not get my new dress dirty. She threatened, if I messed up my dress, I wouldn't be able to attend the reception. I figured this was a veiled threat because I was Mom's "Love," and she wouldn't punish me. My dress ended up a mess and Mom did punish me. She said I was going to have to stay home with my cousin, Donna. I was always afraid of Donna because she was so pale that I thought she was a ghost. I was too young to know that it was just the way God made her as an Albino. After everyone left me at home, I ran down the street chasing Mom's car trying to get away from Donna.

The next week we left for Sacramento. We moved into another very nice house with Dad. The house had a big kitchen at the front of it and bedrooms down the long hallway in the back. Everything was going well until a couple of disturbing events occurred.

One evening Mom was in the kitchen frying chicken and I was sitting on a tall stool keeping her company. My siblings were in the back of the house playing and Dad was in the room sleeping so he could get ready for the night shift at work. Our cousin, Donna, had moved to Sacramento too, but she didn't live with us. On this particular evening she was over visiting. She was supposed to be in the back of the house with my siblings. Mom and I heard a loud, insistent yell from Dad, "MABLE!!!" Mom took off running to their bedroom. I was right behind her. When we arrived there, Dad was yelling at Donna to get out of my parent's bed. Apparently, she had snuck in the bed with my Dad pretending she was Mom. Dad said he only discovered it after a few minutes. Mom kicked Donna out and returned her to the mental institution, which is where she was, apparently, before she came to our house that day.

This was my first time realizing someone could have something wrong with their mind. I didn't know the medical term was mental illness, I just knew this woman had to be out of her mind to climb in bed with my father!

The only other memories I have about living with both of my parents involved many arguments and stress. The fighting seemed to always revolve around Dad having other girlfriends. My siblings and I knew Dad had other girlfriends because he didn't shy away from introducing us to a couple of them whenever we were out and about. Also, he typically bribed us with candy not to talk about our trips with Mom. But one particular evening, I learned of another perspective when we received an unexpected visitor at home. Flowers were delivered. Some beautiful red, long stem roses were delivered to Mom. At the time, I was so enamored with the beautiful roses; I hadn't noticed they were not from Dad. That notification didn't arrive until Dad returned home from work. He walked into the living room, put his feet up on the table where the flowers sat as the center piece, and loudly inquired, "Who died?" It was the answer to this question which started the fight that evening. All I can really remember is trying to hide Dad's gun from Mom. Dad was a police officer, so he always had a gun in the house. Thank God none of us ever hurt ourselves while trying to keep Dad and Mom from hurting each other.

I also recall a Friday evening when Mom took Aunt Glafie, Dad's first cousin, home. I decided to tag along in the backseat. As we rode down the street, I noticed Mom pulled the car over to the side of the road and stopped. Sitting in the back seat, I hadn't noticed what caused this abrupt stop. Then Mom exited the car and walked toward the rear of it. As I stood to look out of my back window, I saw Mom talking to a man in another car. The man was her ex-boyfriend, Jerry. Jerry wasn't supposed to be in Sacramento. All I know is soon after some flowers mysteriously appeared, we saw Jerry, and my parent's divorce proceedings were started.

In the divorce proceedings, my parents decided to split our family in half, if there is such a thing. However, Dad was adamant about telling the judge Hootnanne was not his child. Nevertheless, because Hootnanne resembled Dad even more than all of us other six children (and this was before DNA science), the judge chuckled and exclaimed, "Oh, he's yours, Mr. Ackerson, I can tell." With a hit of the gavel, Dad now had custody of Bull, Mutt, Bolo and Hootnanne. Dig, Hop, and I had to live with Mom.

Hootnanne seemed to take the divorce between my parents the hardest of all the children. Dad never accepted Hootnanne as his son and Mom never told Hootnanne that he had a different father. Part of the problem was we were all made aware Bolo wasn't actually Dad's son because Mom sent Bolo to his natural father's family in Fresno during a summer vacation. When Dad found out, he hit the ceiling. Yet, Dad and Bolo seemed to have an inseparable relationship because of their one-on-one time in Oklahoma. But as for Hootnanne, there was no secret he and Dad just tolerated one another.

As part of the divorce court order we were to see our brothers during the summer months. Although this may have seemed like a good idea to my parents and a judge, it really wasn't. Coming from a family of four boys and three girls, no matter how dysfunctional we were, and being relegated to a family of just Mom and two sisters, except for summers, further disrupted our ability to firmly connect as brothers and sisters.

CHAPTER 7

Give "Love" A Chance

By the time I was six years old, Mom brought my sisters and I back to Bakersfield to be close to her parents again and in search of love from Jerry. Originally, we moved in with Jerry into a ranch style house out in the country on Cottonwood Road. Jerry seemed to be doing all the things Mom wanted him to do, including buying a house, furniture and food. In addition, he took Mom to nice restaurants and really knew how to charm her. Yet, Mom would later say that she had been blind to him because of his flowery words and flamboyance. She also spoke of the fact that she believed he knew he was an important part of her life because he too knew welfare wasn't enough on which to live. Mom said, the money we were receiving from welfare was only enough to keep our heads above water.

In my eyes, things were going smoothly. With Jerry,

we seemed to recapture the look of a family although we missed our brothers. We lived on a farm with many animals including chickens, pigs, cows and horses. Some evenings, Mom called to me outside to bring her a chicken. The first couple of times I brought her a chicken I didn't quite understand what she was doing with it, but I noticed I never returned it outside. Also, we always had chicken for dinner on those evenings. Then, one day after seeing Mom wring a chicken's neck, I chose to never eat a chicken again while living on the farm. Those poor chickens!

Living on the farm had its perils, too. Mom and Hop had at some point accidentally stepped on nails in the backyard requiring them to go to the doctor for a shot. In my immature mind, I was just looking at all the attention surrounding each of their crisis. I didn't really grasp that they made painful mistakes and it was serious business. So, one day when I was outside in the backyard playing around by myself, I decided I wanted to see how it felt to have a nail in my foot. I know it sounds crazy, but I intentionally stepped on a wood board with a nail sticking out of it. I immediately felt this sharp piercing pain. I screamed so loud that Hop came running to my rescue. This was my first introduction to being a follower. I should've learned my lesson, but unfortunately, I didn't.

Mom said in the back of her mind she always wanted to be a journalist. She was involved in a journalist project which allowed her to do an internship at the local station.

Courting with Chance

One of Mom's professors wanted her to do television (TV), so he pitched Mom's name to the local news channel. In a short time, Mom was reporting the news on channel twelve as a Bakersfield College reporter. On Saturdays, we all watched the taped shows, including Jerry. My most exciting memory of Mom working was one night when we saw her on TV reporting the local news. It couldn't have been more than two to three minutes, but it was the proudest moment of our lives to see our mother on TV. To me, Mom was large and in charge. She was in control. So, it was right up her alley to be on TV reporting the evening news. This further convinced me she was smart and talented. I was happy she was my Mom.

Later, Mom was hired by the Bakersfield Californian as a cub reporter and worked there for six months, before she was laid-off because her job had been notified my oldest sister, Dig, was ditching school. Then when Mom's job at the Californian was over, she was hired at the California State College, Bakersfield, as a receptionist. She was glad to be gradually getting off welfare. It was during those two jobs Mom had to pay something out of her pocket to attract good babysitters. Although neither job was permanent, Mom had gotten her feet wet in the work force and the water felt good. During the summer, Mom also worked five days a week as a domestic for the Banks family. She couldn't wait to get home to Dig, Hop and me.

We missed Mom too, but with her gone for a week

at a time, we could get away with stuff which wouldn't happen with her home. For instance, Dig and I played a prank on Grandma Gordon. We always thought she was gullible, so we decided to trick her into believing she had won the Fifty Thousand Dollar Sweepstakes. Dig called Grandma and pretended to be from the sweepstake's company. I was just in the background encouraging Dig to embellish more. Hop on the other hand, had already warned us our trick was cruel and she wanted no part of it. So when Dig slipped and laughed because Grandma Gordon was relentless in saying she didn't want to wait for the check to be mailed, but she was going to call her daughter (Mom) at work to bring her to pick up the check, we knew we were going to be in big trouble once Mom got home. So, Dig and I prepared for a punishment. We put on extra pants to cushion the blow of the belt. Mom didn't believe I would participate in such a cruel trick, so she decided to punish Dig and Hop only. I went into the room and hurried up taking off my extra pants while Mom was occupied whopping Dig and Hop. I really felt sorry for Hop, but not sorry enough to fess up.

Mom was also intent on making us respectable ladies. I remember her words echoing throughout the car or house: "Don't be a whore! Don't let men think you're easy." At my age, I didn't quite know what a whore was, nor did I know what it meant to be easy, but I do remember getting a clear example soon after Mom's talk.

Courting with Chance

One night, Mom and Jerry had a party. One of Mom's girlfriends and another guest decided they were fond of each other and ended up in my bedroom. I walked in my bedroom and noticed the light was out. In the darkness I heard moaning. There was also somebody in my bed moving up and down. I went to tell Mom what I saw. She said, "Oh hell!" Then she went into the kitchen and grabbed the broom. After storming into the room, I heard her say, "Get out of my house! You won't have sex in front of my kids." She took the broom and started swinging all over the place. Then I heard screaming and hollering and saw a man and woman grabbing their clothes and struggling to put them on while ducking from the broom Mom was swinging at them. Mom managed to get in a few licks before they busted out the back door screaming, "Ouch, damn!"

Things seemed to have gone downhill between Mom and Jerry, too. Dig accused Jerry of trying to rape her. At the time, I had no idea of why there was so much chaos. It seemed Mom was angry at Jerry, but she was also angry at Dig. Since Dig is six years older than me, she couldn't have been more than twelve. I remember thinking whatever she did with Jerry to make Mom angry, I certainly wanted to make sure I never did it.

Mom left Jerry and we moved several times in search of stability.

CHAPTER 8

Chance To Prove Myself

I was a bright child who enjoyed talking and writing. Because of Mom's interest in journalism, I was exposed to the power of the written and spoken word early.

As a first grader, I joined the Dr. Martin Luther King Jr. essay contest and wrote an essay entitled, "I am Black, and I am Proud!" I wrote: "I am black, and I am proud! My mother is black, and she is proud! My sisters are black, and they are proud! My dog is black and proud! My cat is black, and it is proud, just like Dr. Martin Luther King Jr. was black, and proud!" I presented it, and yes, I won the first-place prize of twenty dollars. I ran all the way home with my money so Charlotte, the school bully, and her friends wouldn't take it from me.

Courting with Chance

I also knew I was a leader as early as the first grade. Back then stores allowed children to purchase cigarettes for their parents as long as they had a note. Mom was a smoker and I was tasked with buying her cigarettes. One of those times, I saved one of the notes. I decided to buy cigarettes and take them to school. I had a plan with my little best friend, Yvonne Samuel, and other classmates to smoke. We surveyed an area behind the school building, but we didn't anticipate other kids playing tag and running in the back of the building where we were. We knew we were in trouble when they saw us. Yvonne hadn't puffed yet, and the other little girl had a mint, so only Johnny and I were sent to the principal's office. At the time, corporal punishment was still alive and well, so Johnny was swatted with a huge wooden paddle and sent back to class immediately. For some reason the office couldn't find Mom to get permission to swat me at first, so I waited about two hours before getting my swat. It was so painful, but I had a reputation to uphold, so I lied to my classmates. I told them I was just asleep in the principal's office. This was the first time I convinced an entire group to see the world my way.

Furthermore, from watching Bolo defend me against Hootnanne, I learned to defend others, and I had a strong conviction for justice ever since. So, in the second grade, while on the playground, I was offended when I saw Charlotte cut the line in front of little Jessica. I walked right up to Charlotte and announced she wasn't going to get away with bullying Jessica, and I was there to make sure. Charlotte didn't take my threat seriously, so I had to put up my dukes to prove it, and I did. I actually beat up the school bully!

CHAPTER 9

Chance To Meet God

From early on, Mom imparted words of wisdom to my sisters and I. Lessons like: "Go to church, tell the truth, don't steal, do people right, and don't hurt others or proverbs like: You get more bees with honey than vinegar; two hats are better than one, especially when one is made for a hat only; Don't look a gift horse in the mouth; A bird in hand is better than two in a tree; Some people you have to feed with a long-handle spoon; or Don't bite the hand that feeds you."

Mom's words of wisdom helped, but Hop dragging me to church helped even more. Hop and I learned many lessons in church. We also gained a cloak of protection that would take us places in life we never imagined and gave us peace of mind we always prayed for. Church was where we received love, protection and sometimes the necessities of life.

Because Mom was a single mother on welfare, we hardly ever got what we wanted like toys and the latest fashions. Hop found us a church to attend, Saint's Memorial Church of God In Christ (COGIC) pastored by Rev. Eddie McGee. We went to church every time the doors were open. Also, we accepted every challenge and participated in every opportunity. The church was wonderful enough to pick us up and drop us off at home after services. I learned how to speak to groups at church by presenting Easter and Christmas speeches. We also received Christmas gifts from church. It seemed that Mom could only afford one doll for each of us and some school clothes. So, all of our fun toys came from church. I started to hate dolls because Mom bought Dig and Hop black dolls and a white one for me. She probably thought I didn't notice, but I did. So, I just grew up resenting dolls altogether as I could never figure out why I received a different one than my big sisters.

Mom started dating a new man, Chum Steeler. Within months, we were moving from our house to live with Chum. Just after we moved in, we heard a rumor at church that the Ten Commandments were coming on TV. We did not have a TV at Chum's house, so we decided to get one from our grandparent's house.

Hop and I walked to my grandparents to pick it up.

Courting with Chance

It looked too heavy for Hop, but she insisted she could carry it by herself. We even had to cross a ditch in the middle of Brown Street. Once we made it back home to Chums, Hop was in a lot of pain because her wrists were hurting. We watched the Ten Commandments that night and enjoyed it, but it wasn't as memorable as Hop ending up with a huge swelling which turned out to be a hernia on her right wrist. Seeing the hernia was a constant reminder of how faithful she was and how desperate we were to want to watch the Ten Commandments. Our hearts were so pure, and we were so convinced God would rescue us just like he rescued the Israelites.

Living with Chum was also a very volatile time between Mom and Dig. Dig accused Chum of trying to rape her too, but Mom refused to believe Dig. I believed Dig because Chum violated me in the second grade. One day, I came home from school early due to a stomach ache. Chum and his adult son were at the house in the den. I went to my bedroom in the back of the house and lay down to sleep. Chum called for me. When I came to him, he lifted my dress, and began to touch me all over my body. All I could do was stand there terrified because I didn't know what else to do. It wasn't long before Chum sent me over to his son and his son started to do the same thing. I felt helpless and terrified. This was extremely confusing to me because Chum also appeared to encourage my academic success. He spent extra time helping me learn my timetables. Chum did violate me other times when he entered my room in early morning hours. I decided to sleep in my panties so I would know if I had been violated in my sleep. I knew if my panties were not still on me the next morning, I had been violated by Chum.

I never told Mom because I didn't think she would believe me as she didn't believe Dig. It seemed that Dig was getting blamed for everything going wrong in the house already. I never told my sisters because I was afraid for them. I thought it would make them targets.

Hop, however, was always finding creative ways to get us out of the house. In addition to church, she signed us up to work in the fields. We woke up at three o'clock am to go pick peas. This was a way of escape for me and to earn some much-needed money.

One day, I was in the kitchen watching Mom cook while she was chastising Dig. Mom thought Dig was pregnant and was trying to get her to fess up to it. It was at this time, I heard Mom share another proverb, "The dark shall come to the light." About two months later, I recognized the fullness of this statement. I think Mom thought Dig was pregnant by Chum. Dig was pregnant, but not by Chum.

Dig was taken from our home and placed in foster care, which is where I thought I would go if I opened my big mouth.

Soon thereafter, we moved to another house, this time it was just Mom, Hop and I. One day, Mom picked me up from school and drove me to a gas station. She filled a gas can with gas and drove to Chum's house. When we arrived, she exited the car holding the gas can and disappeared. The next time I saw her, she was pouring gas around his house. She then ran and jumped into the car and took off. I never heard anything about Chum again. I was glad.

There was a different type of turmoil in the new house. First, Dig was clearly pregnant at sixteen. Although she was living in a foster home, she visited on the weekends. Mom was very hurt but resigned to the fact Dig was having a baby and Mom was hell bent on trying to keep Hop and me from following Dig's example. Second, Mom decided she was going to stop smoking. She enlisted me and Hop to help her. Mom even gave us permission to stop her from going to the store to buy cigarettes. She actually did well for about three days, then Mom started having withdrawals for a cigarette. When Hop and I kicked into gear and our encouragements failed, we stood tall in front of the door and declared she couldn't leave the house to go to the store to buy cigarettes. This didn't go over too well. Mom flat out threatened to beat us unmercifully if we didn't move from in front of the goddamn door! It was this interaction between me, Hop and Mom which turned me off from smoking cigarettes thereafter. I began to think something was really wrong if a small little stick had so much power over Mom that she would resort to cursing, threats and possibly violence, if we didn't comply with her orders. After this episode, Mom tried to quit many times but wasn't successful until she found black licorice as her antidote about twenty years later.

My sisters and I were taught more stealing techniques courtesy of our brothers during the summers when they came to visit. On one occasion, they broke into our neighbor's houses and cleaned them dry. For some reason, I got in my pea brain I deserved things without earning them. Once my brothers left, my sisters and I started stealing little things too– When our mother gave us money for grocery shopping, we split up the shopping list, and stole everything from Food Basket instead of buying it, then used the money to buy Taco Bell. We did this for several months until our mother showed up unexpectedly one day while we were grubbing down at the Taco Bell next door to Food Basket. When she demanded our grocery receipt, we were busted!

The fact that our mother busted us was enough for Hop. She never stole again to my knowledge but Dig and I were just warming up.

Mom, however, was determined not to have us girls turn out the way she was seeing the boys turn out. So, the next time I stole from a store and Mom found out, she took me back to the store and reported it to the manager. Mom made me return the item and apologize. I was humiliated, but not deterred.

I also recognized the power of my mouth very early from how my siblings reacted to me and I never backed down from a good fight even in the neighborhood.

One day, I got into an argument with some neighbor girls. I don't even remember what we were arguing about, but I was glad to see Dig joined me in support of my defense. Hop, on the other hand, was always Ms. Goodie-too-shoes, so she was just busy telling us to stop arguing and come home. But I was determined to get my point across and felt super secure with Dig having my back.

As we turned to walk back into the house, Hop told me to "come on!" We were basically walking in a line with Hop up front, Dig next then me taking up the rear. I turned around to say one more thing to the "enemy," and simultaneously I saw a stick coming down toward my face. Unfortunately, the stick hit me directly between my eyes. The pain from the hit was unimaginable. The stick had metal hanging from it. I turned and looked at Dig and Hop. Tears were streaming down my face mixing with the blood that was gushing from my forehead. Dig and Hop ran back for me and just started screaming for Mom. I was screaming uncontrollably because of all the blood and I'm sure I looked a scary mess. I was rushed to the hospital along with the piece of wood lying beside me. The doctor said I was lucky not to have lost my left eye.

I took note of how powerful my mouth must have been to cause the vengeance displayed against me.

It seemed that it took forever for my face to heal. I

was hoping it healed before Hop and I were scheduled to go visit Dad in Sacramento that summer. This particular visit was going to be interesting as Dig was not going because she was in her final months of her pregnancy and our brothers were actually coming to visit Mom while we were visiting Dad.

Once Hop and I arrived at Dad's, we learned that Dad and his long-time girlfriend, Ms. Pearl, had a trip planned for us. The four of us traveled to San Francisco on vacation. It was so much fun to ride the cable cars, eat fun food and go to the Zoo. I'll never forget watching Dad tease the gorillas by pretending to be one and making gorilla noises. One of the big gorillas actually picked up some "boo-boo" off the ground and threw it at Dad before giving Dad the middle finger. We all laughed uncontrollably. Hop also got a chance to ride in a helicopter across the Bay area, it looked too scary for me, so I passed. We enjoyed our trip so much that we didn't want to return back to Bakersfield. We were so happy when we phoned home to tell Mom about our trip and found out we were moving to Los Angeles, California, upon our return back to Mom.

CHAPTER 10

Chance For A Better Life

In 1974, Mom decided to move to Los Angeles for a fresh start. I was nine years old at the time. Dig had just given birth to her first child, Shawnie, and she was planning to move with us. Hop and I were excited to leave Bakersfield but scared at the same time. We knew we needed to find a good church, so as soon as we arrived, we were on a mission to find one.

Hop and I sought out a church experience similar to Saints Memorial COGIC in Bakersfield. Try as we might, we just couldn't find one with the right combination of love, inspiration and hope. Nevertheless, while we were searching, we made a pact we would always keep our country values and not get citified in Los Angeles. We swore we would never backtrack to an old boyfriend because of what we witnessed with Mom, too. Finally,

Hop and I pledged to become successful. She wanted to be a nurse, and I wanted to be a doctor, a forensic pathologist. I was still curious about why people died ever since I was five years old and witnessed that woman die in front of me. More than anything, we just didn't want to end up like Mom relying on a no-good man to help ends meet.

We first moved into an apartment complex on Alondra and Compton Avenue in Compton, California. The complex was pretty large considering we had only lived in houses or small apartment units in Bakersfield.

Having been trained to be mannish by my brothers, I found it humorous to teach my friends in the complex how to go to the electrical boxes for the units and turn off lights for the entire complex. After doing it a couple of times and finding great humor in watching the tenants scramble around in the dark, we were caught. Hop discovered it was me. She put a stop to all of our fun.

One evening, my Dad's brother, Uncle Roy and his girlfriend, Aunt Neda, and their friends, were over visiting. They were drinking and having a good time into the wee hours of the night. At some point, they decided to leave, but they failed to recognize it was late and they were too loud. One of the neighbors responded to all the noise and an argument erupted. The argument turned from verbal to physical to gun shots. Bullets were flying everywhere. It was a real shoot out. Thank God nobody was shot.

Courting with Chance

In getting settled in terms of work, Mom was only able to find a couple of dead-end jobs before she returned to domestic work. She first went to work for Lennie Johnson, Mrs. Johnson was the mother of Browne Johnson, a young movie star that was strangled by her boyfriend. Unfortunately, Mom hurt her back on the job. Mom said she was fired while dealing with welfare and seeing doctors for her back.

Mom's back injury intensified, and she couldn't work for six months, yet the people at the welfare office weren't sympathetic. Mom got to a point she couldn't pay rent and her car was repossessed. Mom went to Legal Aid for help. It was a drawn out and difficult process, but Mom finally received the money due to her from welfare.

Mom was still off work receiving treatment for her back injury, when my brothers started migrating to Los Angeles to live with us. Mom couldn't afford to take care of them, but she couldn't refuse them either. Mutt was the first to move to Los Angeles. It wasn't long after Mutt arrived that I noticed he had a problem reading and writing. He came to me to read simple things. For instance, if he met a girl and she wrote her name and phone number on a piece of paper, Mutt couldn't read her name. Plus, I noticed that I never saw him write anything. When I mentioned this fact to Mom, she blamed Mutt's inability to read on Dad. Mom's theory was Dad was responsible because Dad worked at Mutt's high school as part of the school police and the teachers just allowed Mutt to pass grades and graduate without teaching him because they were just trying to get next to Dad.

We moved from the Alondra complex to a bigger house in Compton to make room for Mutt. Our new house was closer to Uncle Roy and Aunt Neda. It was around the corner from Peach Street in a neighborhood known as Fruit Town. This area is best known for the origination of the Fruit Town Piru gang. Peach Street was appealing because you could get any type of alcohol, drug or prostitute there.

Mom even got caught up in the snare of Peach Street for a period. Mom began to change in a way that didn't make sense. She met a guy on Peach Street that she started dating. All I remember about him was he spent the night and slept with Mom. The problem was I still shared a bed with Mom, so that meant he slept with Mom and me. Many nights, I heard and saw Mom having sex next to me. I pretended to be sleep or even invisible.

Peach Street negatively affected my best friend from the Alondra complex, Lori, too. Her mother ended up dating my Dad's cousin, Creno. He also hung out on Peach Street when he visited from Sacramento. Unfortunately, Creno was a bad character with a reputation as a pimp, and Lori's mother was totally naïve to the fast life. It wasn't long before Creno had Lori's mother prostituting, and she abandoned Lori and her brothers. Lori and her brothers ended up moving out of state with their grandmother. My heart was broken. I felt I was responsible for the devastation which overtook Lori's family because it started on Peach Street with my family. I always wondered what happened to them.

While living in Fruit Town, I attended Rosecrans Elementary School in Compton for the fourth grade. I observed my teacher being extra mean to the boys in my class. It seemed she complained about everything they did, so much so that she made me angry. On one particular day I was so irritated I thought I would do something about it. So, I requested the hall pass to go to the bathroom. I took a black marker with me. On the hall pass I wrote: "Mrs. Joseph is a bitch!" Unfortunately, she assumed one of the boys wrote the derogatory note on the hall pass, and all the boys were punished. I didn't fess up. But I did learn I would need to find a positive way to help the helpless.

Most young people learn how to drive at age fifteen and a half. I actually started a little sooner or, I guess a lot sooner than the norm. Dig was my first driving instructor when I was nine years old. As a matter of fact, I drove Mom's car as long as I didn't snitch on Dig for getting high. Sometimes she also let me try a joint, too.

Around twelve years old, I outgrew snitching completely, but somehow my mouth was still always getting me in trouble. I remember Dig wanted to go out on the town and she assumed I would babysit baby

Shawnie. I was adamant I wasn't going to babysit, and she couldn't make me. I said it just a little differently though. I said, "No, I'm not babysitting! I didn't lay down and open my legs to have this baby, why am I going to be stuck with her?" Even though my statement was true, I was obviously too sassy because I ended up getting slapped, backhanded by Mom. I was angry because I didn't realize what I said wrong.

This period was also a pretty crazy time of more financial instability for Mom. We moved into five houses in a two-mile radius in Compton over a couple of years to dodge evictions.

Around this time, I took my first summer trip to Sacramento to visit my Dad and my brothers by myself. It was memorable. Dad had married Ms. Pearl. She was continuing to help dad raise my brothers and dad helped Ms. Pearl raise her granddaughter, Angel. Visiting Sacramento during the alternating summer months was always interesting for me. I observed that Angel was the apple of Ms. Pearl's eye. Angel could do no wrong. However, the obvious was always missed with Angel. My brothers had too much day-to-day involvement with her, which I believe cost Angel her innocence.

Also, Dad was a manager for several family housing units near his home. On one occasion, Uncle Roy and Dad laughed about the heist they got away with. Dad and Uncle Roy set up an inside job to steal the rent payments. Apparently, Uncle Roy wanted to make things look really legit, so he hit Dad in the face with the pistol during the planned robbery. Dad wasn't really happy about Uncle Roy's staging idea. This was just the beginning of ruthless behavior my brothers would learn to model.

The next time I returned to Sacramento, I stayed with my oldest brother, Bull, and his girlfriend, Desdra. They lived at the bottom of a two-story duplex downtown. My younger brother, Hootnanne, and Desdra's younger brother, Jimmy, were my play mates- big mistake! We spent most of our days playing around the yard, including disturbing a bee nest. Hootenanne would put me on his shoulders with a broom and I would hit the nest, drop down and run to the upstairs stairwell behind a door. It was so much fun until one fateful day. After hitting the nest, I jumped off Hootnanne's neck to run to my normal hiding place. Unfortunately, after I reached the stairwell, as I closed the door behind me, I realized several bees had followed me. I got stung all over. It felt like I was stung by almost twenty bees.

After I healed, we had to find some other form of excitement. Hootenanne and Jimmy suggested we look for valuables in the cars parked near the State Capitol. Generally, people didn't leave much in sight, but every now and then we would come across something worth breaking a window for.

We had done this for a couple of days before the State Police wised up to our shenanigans. On one particular day out of the blue, a cop on a motorcycle came toward us. I was the lookout, so I warned Hootnanne and Jimmy. We ran as fast as we could. Hootnanne was caught, but Jimmy and I made it home safely. We were hiding when we heard a knock at the door. Apparently, the cops thought they were looking for two boys because I wore braids close to my head. Hootnanne hadn't snitched on us. The cops had followed us. They did come into the house and got Jimmy. Unfortunately, he had no loyalty to me, and he snitched me out. But, luckily for me, the cops didn't come back.

Dad was so angry when he found out about this. He whipped Hootnanne like nobody's business. I didn't get whipped, but I was scared to death!

Returning back to Moms was crazy too. Dig was again out of Mom's house, so things got even tighter probably because less money was being received from welfare. It was so tight for Mom financially that one weekend Hop and I found ourselves on the doorsteps of a girl's delinquent shelter. Most of the girls were there because they were in trouble. Hop and I knew we weren't in trouble, but we also knew Mom had no way to feed us so we stayed in the facility for what felt like an eternity until Mom returned for us. I clung to Hop like crazy while in the shelter. After we returned to our everyday lives, I started hanging out with Dig again because I was still intrigued by her sense of adventure.

One time, I asked Mom to buy me a panty and bra set because I thought I needed it. I felt extra poor because I thought Mom couldn't afford underwear for me. Mom laughed and said she would think about it. My sisters and I went shopping at the cost-effective store at the time, Zody's Department Store. As we shopped, Dig and I came up with a plan to steal. I decided to steal a panty and bra set for myself and Dig asked me to steal something for baby Shawnie. I placed the items at the bottom of Shawnie's stroller. Dig and I were both caught and taken into the security office. Hop didn't know where we were, and she was walking around the store crying. Eventually security figured out she wasn't in on our plan and they told her where we were being held. They told us we were being detained and taken to juvenile hall. They took us to the police station and placed us in separate rooms. Dig was smart enough to give the police Uncle Roy's phone number and not Mom's. We would've been ok with Uncle Roy and Aunt Neda picking us up, but Uncle Roy was drunk when he arrived at the police station. He cursed out the police. They ended up releasing us to Aunt Neda and keeping Uncle Roy until he sobered up.

Having the embarrassment of being detained at Zody's and Uncle Roy's debacle should have been enough to derail me from stealing, but it still wasn't.

That summer, Hootnanne came to visit. One day while we were shopping in the Wonder Bread store on Rosecrans Avenue in Compton, we stole some of the food stamp change slips. The slips were designed to be used by customers who obtained change after using food stamps. Once we got the slips home, we doctored them up and returned to the store to use them in exchange for sweets galore. We actually got away with using the slips for about two weeks, but our scheme came to a screeching halt one afternoon because Hootnanne went one step too far. He actually thought the slips would look more authentic, if he included an employee's initials on them. Unfortunately, he didn't know the names of any of the actual employees, so just placing arbitrary initials on the slips was a dead giveaway. They discontinued the use of the slips. Hootnanne left the following week to return to Sacramento. I was glad to see him go.

CHAPTER 11

Painful Chance

J ust recently I drove down Compton Blvd leaving
work at the Compton Courthouse and turned
right on Wilmington Avenue. Typically, this route is
embraced with glimpses of my past, but this particular
trip was different because I had a passenger. My
passenger was one of my colleagues, Honorable Laura
Walton.

As I drove, I spontaneously pointed out familiar
landmarks. "See the house right there on the corner, the
beige one that sort of looks like a business? I used to
live there." Then turning to my right, I directed her to
look east on Poplar Street to point out another house in
the middle of the block. Then I turned my attention to
the schools. "I attended both of those schools too,
Dickerson Elementary and Davis Junior High. We lived
in several more places here in Compton

too." Somehow that conversation played back to me several times since that day. The playback version included more details and a stream of emotions I thought were long gone. Life itself has a funny way of keeping you honest. For some odd reason, you can't run and/or hide from your own stream of consciousness.

As I remembered my experiences on Poplar Street, I couldn't help but wonder how the story unfolded for my fifth-grade friend, Rama.

Rama was my ace on Poplar Street. She lived with her Mom. Rama had dark chocolate smooth skin, thick black hair and a fun spirit. I have two life-altering memories of Rama. One is the time when Rama talked me into ditching school with her to go home for lunch. We just wanted to live on the edge and go eat at home. So, once we left school, we were just chatting it up on our way to Rama's house. Upon arriving at her house, we stood in front of her front door while she searched for the house key. As I stood there, I heard a still, quiet voice whisper to me, "move over." As if the command came from someone standing in front of me, I moved slightly over to my left, just to the side of the door. Shortly thereafter, Rama found the key, inserted it into the lock and proceeded to open the front door. Much to our dismay and fright, right as Rama opened the door; her mother was standing in the door shaking while pointing a gun toward us. As we yelled, "Oh my God!" she just began to cry hysterically. Once we calmed her down, we found out she thought we were burglars.

Courting with Chance

Rama's house had been burglarized the week prior, and her Mom thought the burglars were returning with a key. As she continued to sob, she told us she would've shot the gun, but she stopped short of pulling the trigger because she saw a familiar colored article as the door opened slightly. She saw my trademark hot pink windbreaker. I shudder to think of the outcome had I not listened to that still, low voice to move over so my hot pink windbreaker was visible.

The second life-altering memory still plagues me today, forty years later, and it also motivates me to help the wounded and hurting get to the root of their pain and triumph over it in my drug court every day.

It was a beautiful sunny day in Compton. Rama and I were playing tetherball at our favorite hangout across the street. We normally played for hours because it was fun, fast and close to home, so it was supposed to be safe. I ran across the street to my house to use the bathroom. When I entered the house, my eighteen-year old brother, Mutt, was there. As I left the bathroom, he approached me and asked me to ask Rama if she wanted $20. So, I went back outside to the tetherball court and said, "Rama, do you want $20?" Of course, she said, "Yes!" Then I told her to go into the house to see Mutt and he would give it to her, if she did him a favor. In total innocent oblivion, Rama skipped across the street to my house. I continued to play tetherball alone for nearly an hour before Rama returned outside. We never spoke of what happened. We didn't have to.

I knew because I had been asked to do Mutt a favor many times before.

The first time was when we lived down the street. Mom was working and Hop was gone to visit our cousins at Mom's brother, Uncle Bob's house. Uncle Bob was always financially well off after graduating college and playing professional football for the San Francisco 49ers. He was also appointed as the public relations officer for Governor Ronald Reagan. Uncle Bob allowed Hop to come to his house and spend time with his daughters, which was great because Hop was exposed to a totally better way of life. Hop did everything she could to expose me to that better way too, even though I was fighting her all the way. Most of my resistance was because I felt safe when Hop was around, and I knew when she was gone; I was left with Mutt and Dig because Mom was still working live-in jobs.

Dig's looking out for me took many forms. Sometimes it meant she and I went driving and I got high with her. Other times, it was me waiting for her in the car when she went partying at the motorcycle club. I sometimes ended up in the front seat while she and some goof ball made out in the back seat.

Only Dig, baby Shawnie, and Mutt were home this particular night. The house was dark and quiet. I had gone to bed, when I heard a noise next to me. I came out of the fog of sleep; Mutt was lying next to me naked. I actually couldn't believe my eyes and was shocked, but I didn't know what to do or say. So, I said something like, "What are you doing here like that?" He responded, "I need a favor. I went to Dig for help, but she told me she couldn't help me because she was still bleeding from having the baby, so she told me to come to you." I didn't know what to do. I thought I had to have sex with him because he said, Dig said it was ok. It never occurred to me to ask Dig if she said that because I was so confused. Also, because of my previous experience with Chum and his son, I had a weird twisted feeling it was my responsibility to be an object to help men with my body regardless of how I felt about it. So, after that night, Mutt visited my room weekly for a favor over the next year. I often found reasons to spend the night away at a friend's house just to avoid the weekly ritual, but I never told anyone because I felt ashamed.

Then in my sick, twisted childish mind, I thought I found a way to help my brother and myself. So, I gave him Rama and totally put the entire incident out of my mind because I didn't want to think I betrayed my childhood friend to the same wolf to whom I believed my sister betrayed me.

CHAPTER 12

Chance To Learn Lessons

Mutt finally got a girlfriend and I was happy because I thought it meant he would leave me alone. He was dating Marion. Marion was a little older than Mutt and she already had two children. Meanwhile, Mutt was also dating Tammy, a sixteen-year old neighbor. Tammy's mother was on drugs and her father was in prison, so she lived with her grandmother, Nana. Nana worked really hard to be strict and keep Tammy on the straight and narrow path, but Tammy was resistant at every turn. Tammy had just announced she was pregnant with Mutt's child.

One Saturday night, both women showed up for Mutt's birthday party. Everybody was having a good time. I was in charge of cutting the cake. After singing happy birthday, I was getting ready to cut the cake. All of a sudden, Marion grabbed the knife from my hand

and yelled, "I'll kill that bitch!" I didn't realize who she was talking about until I ran after her to retrieve the knife and saw her heading toward Tammy. Somebody intervened and talked Marion down from stabbing Tammy, boy was I relieved. Meanwhile, Mutt had snuck out to his friend's car and was drunk as a skunk throwing up profusely.

I remember thinking it was so sad these two women were fighting over him, and he wasn't interested in either of them at the moment. Mutt was too self-engrossed in his drunken state. Unfortunately, respect for my own body was a harder lesson to obtain. I didn't know how to say no because I didn't know I had a right to say no. I was so confused for so long.

CHAPTER 13

Chance To Be Safe

I attended Raymond Avenue Elementary school in Los Angeles for my sixth-grade year with my cousin, Karen Simon, instead of the neighborhood elementary school around the corner from our new house in the Nickerson Garden Projects in Watts, California. Karen was the only girl in a family of eight. Her mother, Louise, was widowed by her father, Rayfield, who was my Dad's first cousin. Rayfield had been murdered a couple of years earlier. Louise and Mom became confidants once we moved to Los Angeles. Also, because Karen and I shared the same name, and our birthdays are twelve days apart, we were inseparable. Mom thought it would be safer for me to attend school with Karen. Unfortunately, Mom didn't know the threat was in our house, because I was still enduring Mutt's sexual coercion over me.

Courting with Chance

Raymond Avenue was on the other side of town, so I had to catch the Rapid Transit District (RTD) city bus. I always found reasons to get home as late as possible to avoid Mutt. Also, Nickerson's Garden Projects was quite overwhelming with lots of people in a very congested area. Children often ran around unsupervised, including me. I had a lot of friends who lived within a couple of doors of us. Drugs were easy to come by, so my friends and I spent a lot of time chilling and getting high on weed on the weekends. We left home in the mornings and headed to the department stores in Huntington Park. We shoplifted until our hearts were content, then returned home and got high laughing about our adventures.

Newberry's Department Store on Central and Rosecrans was my spot to steal fingernail polish. One evening, I walked into Newberry's and I immediately put a couple of knickknacks in my pockets. Once I realized I was being watched, I ran out of the store and took off with all the stuff in my pockets. I decided to hide in the utility cabinet behind the store. Suddenly, I heard voices and I crotched down. I heard one of the guys say, "Did you see her run? She ran as fast as a jackrabbit. I'm sure she's not back here in this electrical cabinet, because she'll be electrocuted, but I'll check it just in case." I was in there shaking my butt off. I was actually relieved when the security guard reached in and grabbed me out.

Mom had to come pick me up from the police station. Once I got home, she called me into the kitchen. I wasn't sure what she wanted, but I soon found out. She called me into the kitchen and asked me for my fingers. She said, "I bet you won't steal another thing." She proceeded to take my fingers and place them over the open fire on the stove until they burned. As my fingers burned, I was furious! I was angrier that Dig was standing there signaling to Mom and saying that I wasn't feeling it, than I was because my fingers were burning. It was painful, but I was doing my very best not to show I was in pain. My poker face backfired and I just let my emotions show, if for no other reason than to save my fingers. Also, I was angry because Dig had conspired with me to steal at Zody's and she encouraged me to steal on most of our adventures but now I was the one getting punished. It was at this instant, I decided not to ever follow someone else to do something crazy. If I was going to do crazy, it was going to be done because it was my crazy idea, as I was the leader, not a follower of the crazy pack anymore.

After deciding to become the leader of the pack I thought I was invincible and actually turned into a bully. On one occasion, my crew and I were walking down the street trying to find something to do, and we spotted two girls we didn't know. We approached them, and I started talking big and bad, which inevitably turned into a fight. Unfortunately, I didn't realize how close I was to the curb, and I slipped and hit my head on it. I literally saw stars! This was the last fight I was involved in as leader or follower. I learned my lesson.

One evening I stayed too long at my Cousin Karen's house near my school. Once I got on the bus to head home, I knew I couldn't beat the darkness. I felt nervous because I didn't want to walk through the projects by myself at night. Just as I was about to exit the RTD bus, I felt a weird kind of comforting feeling I had never sensed before. It was as if someone was praying for me and God was letting me know a prayer came up to heaven with my name on it. Further, in that instance, I imagined I would only find out who the prayer warrior was after I died and made it to heaven.

As I exited the bus, I walked across Central Avenue. I walked toward the elementary school at the entrance to the projects and, as I neared it, I felt a dark presence close to me. When I looked around, I noticed a man following me. He startled me, but I tried to play it cool. He said, "You have nice breasts." I froze because I didn't know how to respond. I was just trying to think of how I was going to get away from this pervert, and I remembered the prayer I felt when I exited the bus. In an instant, a car drove up and flashed its bright lights on us. It was just enough light for me to take off running across the street, and I ran all the way home. I got away and never ever came home late again. Nevertheless, I'll always remember that day as the day I felt someone praying for me. I also realized if that person's prayers saved me that night, I could pray for others the same way. Since then, I pray for people as I encounter them on the streets because I truly recognized the power of prayer that day.

A couple of days later, I took a bike ride down to the park. On my way home, I was riding north on Central against traffic. As soon as I got to 103rd Street, right in front of the County building, I felt a hard hit. I was hit by a car. The driver kept driving as if he didn't realize he hit me. He dragged me for about forty feet before he stopped. Once he stopped and exited his car, he got out to check and saw me and my bike under his car. I was bruised up and in a lot of pain. My bike and I were too banged up to ride it home, so the driver took me and my bike home. Once we arrived, he explained to Mom what happened and left his work information for her. He was apologetic and concerned. Thank God he wasn't a rapist or fool, because he could've dumped me anywhere after I got in his car. I was just grateful to still be alive. I thought of the prayer on the bus again.

Nearing the end of my recovery, I had a follow up doctor's appointment. Mom picked me up early from school for the appointment. I needed to return a library book, so I asked her to take me to the local library. When we arrived at the library on Vermont and Vernon in Los Angeles, I exited Mom's car with my book in hand. As I walked up the stairs to the front door of the library, I noticed it was closed. Simultaneously, I heard police sirens. Just as I turned to look for an overnight slot, there was a man running up to me with a knife in his hand. He scared the crap out of me, and for that second, I didn't know what to do. Fortunately, he was trailed by several Los Angeles police officers (LAPD). He came really close to me and I froze. He looked as if he was deciding to grab me or not, and one of the officers, with his gun drawn, said, "Don't even think about it!" The assailant had a quick decision to make. He dropped the knife and took off running. Whew!!! I couldn't believe it. I was so shaken when I reached Mom's car, I was speechless. God had just saved me from another near disaster. Wow!!!

Then within the year, God orchestrated a situation where I was able to move away. I jumped at the opportunity to get away from Mutt.

CHAPTER 14

Challenging Chance

I moved to San Jose, California, with Mom's youngest brother, Uncle Pinkey, and his wife, Aunt Ora, along with their four children. While living with them, I was exposed to a totally new living and learning environment. At home, having a mother (Aunt Ora) there all the time, while living in a middle-class neighborhood, was really refreshing. It seemed Mom had worked out an agreement to allow me to live with them because I was such a good student and they thought I could be a good influence on their daughter, Ronda. But Ronda and her brothers were extremely spoiled and ungrateful. It was unbelievable for me to watch their entitlement attitudes at work. I totally realized the gains I had received by coming into their household, and I wasn't interested in risking them for anyone. I decided to never get high again and not to steal anymore. I was determined to stay focused.

While living in San Jose, I gained a new perspective on education, too. Although I had always been eager to learn, I realized once I settled into the San Jose School District that I was unprepared. When I left Davis Junior High School in Compton at the end of the first semester of the 7th grade, I was upset I had missed one point on an open book test of the USA states and capitols. In contrast, Piedmont Middle School in San Jose was challenging me to read a novel weekly and learn words like nonchalant and naïve. Piedmont's curriculum was truly preparing me for the standardized test world to come. My student body experience also changed from 90% African American at Davis to 90% Caucasian at Piedmont. I asked my cousin, Ronda, "How can you tell one white person from the other? They all look alike!" I was so ignorant!

I also remember my English teacher at Piedmont being very circumspect of my work. Apparently, her daughter was in my class too and my teacher certainly didn't want me to outshine her daughter. I took all of it as a challenge. I made it my business to work hard, so I couldn't be excluded from opportunities which were based on academic achievement. I was also always industrious. Once I got into the swing of school, I decided to get a job. I bought some 3X5 index cards and advertised babysitting for .75 cents per hour. I ended up with three babysitting jobs.

Approximately one year after I arrived, Uncle

Pinkey's family moved from San Jose to a little town closer to Bakersfield called Hanford. In Hanford, I found the curriculum more closely aligned with San Jose. So, I geared up for the fun of the challenge.

The summer after my seventh-grade year, I returned home from San Jose to visit Mom and I brought along Ronda and her little brother, Rodney. I quickly realized too much was going on in and around Mom's house. I could've easily ended up pregnant or on drugs even though Mutt was gone. Thank God he had moved with a girlfriend.

Mom had moved into a back house on El Segundo Boulevard just east of Wilmington in Compton. A boy named Norris lived in one of the front houses. We had eyes for each other. One night while everyone was sleep, Norris came over. We started smooching and grinding on the couch and time got away from us. We looked up and realized it was about four o'clock in the morning. We heard Mom walking through the house. I played sleep on the sofa and Norris hid next to the chair near the front door. Whew, we were almost busted! I was back to the fast life again.

We also saw drug abuse all around us. Angel dust, Sherm and LSD were the drugs of choice. It was typical to see grown men getting high, hallucinating and jumping off buildings, running into the middle of the streets head on into cars. It was crazy especially for

Ronda and Rodney because they had never seen such things. I was somewhat use to the crazy environment since I had experienced Peach Street.

At the end of the summer, I was happy to return to Hanford. But, during the school year, I noticed living with my uncle and aunt was becoming a financial strain on them. Mom wasn't sending any money for my care and I overheard conversations that my uncle was taking care of two families. It made me really uncomfortable and at some point, I decided I had to leave because I didn't want to be a burden to them. Also, I found out that Mom had moved into another house away from Norris and Mutt was still gone. So, I asked Mom if I could return home. She was hesitant because she knew she couldn't be home with me during the week. Hop was away studying at University of Seattle, Washington in her first year of college. Also, Mom knew she couldn't count on Dig because Dig had just given birth to another baby, Darrin, and she wasn't reliable. After we discussed it, Mom agreed I could return home, but I would have to take care of myself while she was working. I knew I could as long as I didn't have to deal with Mutt. Once I returned home, I lived at home by myself during the week while Mom worked Monday through Friday. I attended Bret Harte Junior High School. Having returned from San Jose and Hanford, school in the inner city of Los Angeles was a piece of cake. Plus, it was a pretty uneventful year because I made sure I was under the radar. In terms of home, things were a lot more exciting because I had absolutely no supervision except when Dig would appear for a couple of hours, during the week to tell Mom she was looking out for me. It was very important for me to keep quiet about living alone so Mom wouldn't get into trouble and also so I could remain safe. Monique, my neighbor and classmate, was the only person who knew. I had sworn her to secrecy so she wouldn't even tell her mother.

Mom was back working for entertainers primarily. She then went to work for Turner Mizer, a writer and cheap skate as Mom put it. At one point, he wanted Mom to reduce her hourly rate with the promise he would help educate me. Mom told him to pay her money because I was a straight "A" student, and as long as there were government grants, she knew I would be ok. Mom said, if he was too cheap to pay for her hourly wages, then why would she expect him to educate her daughter?

Thereafter, Mom took another domestic job with James Boxer and Riser Love, entertainers in television and music. Mom cleaned their home and cared for their two children, Jazzy and Beverly. As their housekeeper, they trusted Mom. Also, often I babysat the girls on weekends when Mom was off duty.

One particular weekend I took the city bus to the San Fernando Valley to babysit the kids while Riser prepared for an upcoming concert. We were all in the studio along with Riser and her band members for rehearsal. At the lunch hour, Riser gave me money to go across the street to Jack in the Box to buy lunch. I purchased everything she requested. Unfortunately, she didn't give me money for myself, and I didn't ask for money because I had too much pride. So, Riser, the girls and the band members ate. I didn't. Certainly, I was with Riser to do a job, babysit. But the fact that I was only thirteen years old should have been enough information for her to care about my eating too.

I overheard Mom saying that Riser and James were getting a divorce. Soon after, the couple separated and James moved out, but Mom had agreed to still work for both of them. About a month later, James called me to come babysit one weekend. After I arrived at his new beach house, Riser showed up for dinner. After the girls and I finished eating, we left James and Riser at the dinner table. I cleaned the kitchen and put the girls to sleep before heading to the guest room. I awoke early the next morning to a clicking noise. Upon leaving the guest room to investigate the noise, I walked into the living-room and stumbled upon James taking pictures of women's underwear tossed about the room. Not really sure what to make of the situation, I just turned around and went back into the guest room before he saw me. Once I heard the girls awake, I came into the kitchen to prepare breakfast for the girls. It was only then that I realized that Riser was still in the house, back in James' room. She had spent the night. I surmised that James was going to try to use the pictures in their upcoming divorce proceedings. Seeing James and Riser's antics made me keenly aware of the behind the scene lives of entertainers after the applause, crowd and lights were off. I realized that they were just normal people with problems like everyone else.

One weekend Mom came home from Riser's whispering about jewelry. Apparently, Mom stole some expensive jewelry from Riser, then Mom traveled to Las Vegas to pawn it. Once they returned from Vegas, Mom gave me lots of nickels. I was so conflicted. I knew Riser never suspected Mom, but I knew she did it, and I was very ashamed. I also witnessed Mom and my brothers planning a staged slip and fall accident in a grocery store. I expected this behavior from my brothers, but not Mom. These behaviors further solidified my decision to not be a thief because thieves could not be trusted, and I started to value trust.

CHAPTER 15

Fiery Chance

While Hop was away in college, she was assigned a roommate from Los Angeles, Eugenie. Eugenie and her parents attended Ephesians COGIC in Los Angeles. After Hop returned home, she was excited to visit the Ephesians church because she still hadn't found a church to her liking since we moved from Bakersfield.

During the period Hop was home, Mom traveled up north on the Greyhound bus and some mechanical problem came up with the bus, which caused a minor fender bender. Mom wouldn't let it go and decided to sue Greyhound. Hop and I were in the car with Mom while she was discussing money, she was hopeful to receive from the lawsuit. Hop mumbled under her breath, "Mom, you sue everybody." I actually said it out loud, "Mom, you sue everybody!" Then I felt a slap on my mouth when Mom backhanded me. Mom responded, "Shut up, that's how I take care of you!" I actually instantly gained another visual that gave me insight – You shouldn't sue people unless they really hurt you.

Fortunately for me, but unfortunately for Hop, she couldn't afford to return to college in Seattle, so she decided to stay home and join Ephesians church. I visited the church with her on a couple of occasions, but I wasn't really sold on rejoining church since I was still hanging out with Dig while Hop was gone. Dig's world seemed much more exciting, at least until one Saturday afternoon.

Saturday was the day Hop and I went to the laundry mat. On this particular Saturday our neighbor's Monique and Cheryl, joined us. Mom remained home to care for Dig's kids: five-year old, Shawnie, and her little brother, Darrin. We were at the laundry mat about one hour, when we heard sirens and saw fire trucks turning the corner near the laundry mat. I just had a sixth sense they were heading to our house, so I said it out loud, but in a matter of fact tone, "I bet they're going to our house." The others just shirked off my comment. Then about five minutes later, Cynthia, Monique and Cheryl's mother, pulled up to the laundry mat blowing her horn to tell us we needed to come home because our house was on fire. We jumped into her car and headed home. We were grateful to find our mother, Shawnie, and Darrin safe on the sidewalk in front of the house. But much to our chagrin, the house appeared to be a total loss, with the exception of the clothes we were washing at the laundry mat. Apparently, Shawnie started the fire playing with incense and a lighter under the bed. It was only after the fire was put out, that we realized Hop's closet was somehow left standing. She was quick to remind us inside her closet was her Bible with a one hundred-dollar bill in it. Hop's testimony was enough to convince me she was on the right track and I needed to reevaluate my loyalties to Dig because Hop and her Jesus seemed to be the safest shelter.

The fire that destroyed our home and picture memories was enough fire for a lifetime for me. I decided I was not going to hell. I accepted Christ as my Lord and Savior that day. Thereafter, I started going to church with Hop and really took the religious stuff serious.

After receiving help from the Red Cross, we lived between hotels and motels for a couple of weeks. Mom decided to move us in with Dig temporarily. Dig, her two children, her boyfriend and Mutt were all living together. They lived on 83rd and Broadway in a three-bedroom apartment in an alley. Mom still worked live-in jobs, so she was only home on the weekends.

Hop and I were unfortunately stuck in Dig's world. The neighborhood was infested with prostitutes, pimps, drugs and filth. Plus, Hop and I were estranged from Dig and the others because we were viewed as Jesus freaks and traitors. They acted like they were scared of us, which was totally alright with me because my Jesus kept Mutt from ever violating me again. They called us freaks because we were so focused on following the rules of our church. We didn't even wear pants or lipstick. We were also treated as traitors because we gave offerings in church rather than giving it to them for drugs. And, we told everyone we came into contact with about Jesus, so they hated talking to us. Additionally, while Mom was away during the week, they would get high in front of us or not let us eat at all by locking up the food in the shelves and the refrigerator. At first Hop and I didn't quite know what to do, so we just prayed and asked God to help us. Miraculously, food always came. Either someone from church would feed us, give us unsolicited monetary gifts or we would be on a fast of dedicating quiet time to God, while choosing not to eat at all, or selecting certain foods or activities to avoid during that time. The purpose was to really make sure we had a clear, uncluttered line of communication with God.

One time, we actually felt like we hit the j a c k p o t because we were hungry, and Hop received her eighteen-hundred-dollar income tax return. We ate well for months. Everybody else in the house was angry with us. Also, on Sunday mornings, Eugenie's parent's, Mr. and Mrs. Thomas, picked us up for church, fed us and returned us home. When they were unavailable, my church friend, Sharon Gill, would get her sister, Barbara McNally, a single mother of three, to pick us up. In addition, I noticed a young man, Mathis Scribe, was always willing to give us a ride home. He was infatuated with Hop.

During that same summer the RTD bus was on strike, which meant Hop and I were relegated to walking whenever we couldn't find a ride. Dig and the gang made it clear we couldn't expect any rides from them. Dig's apartment was at 83rd and Broadway and our church was located on 132nd and Avalon. It was the summer of revivals, continuous nightly church meetings with guest ministers.

Hop and I decided to walk. It didn't matter that the church was at least forty-nine blocks and the heat felt like it was one hundred degrees, what mattered was we were bound and determined to get there. God always provided us a way home. Mathis, Hop's admirer, eventually became our personal chauffeur. I liked to tease Hop by saying, "Mathis likes you. He wants to marry you. You're going to marry chicken." I called him chicken because he was so skinny.

Six months later, Mom found us another place to live. We moved to a duplex on Orchard Street in Los Angeles. It was two bedrooms, but we were bound and determined to make it work for me, Mom, Hop, and Hootnanne. Hootnanne ran away from juvenile hall in Sacramento and came to Los Angeles. Mom turned him in to the authorities and after completing an additional stint in juvenile hall, Hootnanne returned to live with us. While living with us, he got caught burglarizing our neighbor's house. The break-in was enough for our landlord to evict us and he served Mom with an eviction notice. But, because the house was classified as substandard since the heater and hot water heater wasn't working, Mom obtained help from Loyola Law School. Mom took me with her to the free legal clinic at Loyola. Once the matter went to court, Mom said the landlord walked into court with a walking stick for the blind to gain sympathy. It didn't work. Mom won the trial and the owner had to return her deposit.

Also, Mom and I went to the juvenile court for Hootnanne's court appearance. It was my first time in court. The only thing I noticed was that the person in the black robe was in control of everybody in the courtroom. I thought, "I want that job."

CHAPTER 16

Chance For Deliverance

By this time, I was tired of moving. It felt like Mom just couldn't become stable. Hop and I, however, continued to stay focused on church. We spent every Sunday and many weekday nights at Ephesians. One Sunday evening, we had a revival with a guest speaker, Evangelist Ella Davis. Evangelist Davis was the first woman evangelist I ever met. She kept my attention the whole time as she ministered from the Bible. She also had a special gift of healing. During the revival, she called Hop up to the altar to pray for her healing. Specifically, Evangelist Davis indicated God was going to heal the hernia on Hop's wrist. (This was Hop's old injury from carrying the TV for us to watch the Ten Commandments.) Evangelist Davis prayed for the hernia to be removed. About a week later, we noticed the hernia had disappeared and never returned. Again, I thought about the power of prayer.

One day a couple of months later, I was singing in the choir. Singing my heart out, I might add, because singing isn't my forte, but I was filling an empty choir seat. Our church had another visiting minister who was introduced as Apostle Wilcox. Apostle Wilcox visited our church before and was known for his gift of prophecy which involved telling someone their future, as told by God for God's glory. On this particular day, I was sitting in the choir stand after we finished a song, and Apostle Wilcox summoned me to come down to the altar. Once I reached the altar, he placed a small vial of "anointed oil" in my hand and told me God wanted me to take the oil home, wait until everyone was sleep and place it upon the door knobs, while praying simultaneously. He further stated God was going to deliver me. Hearing this was really strange, but I had been at this church long enough to have witnessed stranger things, so I figured I had nothing to lose. I also believed if God didn't say it, we would all know soon enough because nothing would manifest. So, once I arrived home, I did just as Apostle Wilcox said once Mom, Hop and Hootnanne went to sleep.

The very next day was my fourteenth birthday. I was at home helping Mom clean the house. While outside placing clothes on the clothesline, I heard the telephone ring. Mom came to the door and told me the caller identified herself as Mother Curry, the church mother at Ephesians. She was calling to see if I would come to clean her house. I immediately replied, yes, because I knew this was another way to make some extra money besides my babysitting and tutoring of elementary school kids.

Mother Curry picked me up about an hour later and we headed straight to her house. The first person I met when I entered was her five-year old granddaughter, Danielle. She and I started a conversation and Danielle was mystified to discover it was my birthday and I wasn't at home having a birthday party. She was so disturbed. She couldn't wait to introduce me to her mother, Claudia, and share my plight with her.

Claudia was in her third year of law school at University California at Los Angeles (UCLA) School of Law. In conversation with her, she found out I tutored children in addition to doing housework on the weekends, so she asked me if I would tutor Danielle. I agreed to tutor Danielle during the week and clean the Curry's house on the weekends.

So thereafter, during the week, I left Bret Harte Jr. High and caught the bus and picked up Danielle at K. Anthony's Elementary School in Inglewood. We headed to the Curry's and I gave Danielle a snack, helped her with homework and prepared her for bed, before I headed home. Then on Saturday, I always returned to clean the house. This rhythm went on for about six months, before I became really comfortable around the Curry house. All of a sudden, I was spending the night and getting dropped off at school on Monday mornings. As I spent more time, I really began to feel like I was part of the Curry family. Having the safety and security of a Christian family was life-altering to me.

Dad Curry, who we affectionately called Papa, was a consummate gentleman and truly a father, who was also a quiet and unassuming man, who took pride in caring deeply for his family. Outside of family time, he worked for the City of Los Angeles, proudly worshipped at First African Methodist Episcopal Church (FAME) in Los Angeles, and spent his spare time participating in the Grand Lodge.

Mother Curry was a firecracker, who was known fondly as Granny or Mother. She was truly the matriarch of the Curry bunch. Very strong, dignified and smart as a whip. She loved giving back to the community as a foster grandparent and in her role as church mother for Ephesians, then later as a State mother of our church's state jurisdiction. She also found joy in spreading God's word on her weekly radio broadcast on KTYM.

Papa and Granny birthed five children: Hazel, James, Claudia, Robert and Lanette.

Hazel is mild mannered and focused like Papa. She chose to become a schoolteacher and she has accomplished much in the Los Angeles School District. In addition to a regular teaching credential, Hazel also obtained a special education credential and special benefits for being bilingual. Hazel birthed two daughters: Kim and Mari. Hazel is also married to Howard.

Courting with Chance

James is the second oldest. He lived in the Inland Empire with his twin sons: Kevin and Kelvin. Around the time I joined the family, James seemed to bear the burden of being the black sheep of the family because of his issues with alcohol seeming to result from his Vietnam experience while serving in the US Army. James dedicated his life to Christ and married Ruth before leaving California and moving to Colorado, and later to Louisiana.

Claudia, the middle daughter, is like a big sister and mother to me all wrapped up in one person. She taught me so much, especially during my teenage years. First, she even helped bring me to the realization that wearing pants and make-up were man's rules, not God's rules. She taught me to see the church with balance, not reckless abandonment.

I so looked up to Claudia as I watched her intently during her final months at UCLA and while she studied to pass the California State Bar. Unfortunately, she had a difficult time passing the Bar. I was also at home with her on the date when she read in the newspaper that she was a part of a lucky, but not so lucky, original group of law students who were told they did not pass the Bar, but had actually passed. Apparently, the Bar changed the pass range without giving notice because more students than they had originally anticipated passed the test. I'll never forget Claudia's surprise and excitement of finding out she was in that number.

Claudia birthed one daughter: Danielle.

Robert is the youngest son. He was called to the ministry. Robert traveled a lot for the ministry, but when he was in Los Angeles, he lived with Granny and Papa, too. He also modeled for me a true brother-sister relationship. Later, Robert married Barbara and moved to Pittsburgh, Pennsylvania, where they raised one son, Jonathan.

Lanette is the Curry's youngest child, and by virtue of her birthing order, the most difficult to accept my presence originally. Lanette was about twenty-four years old when I arrived on the scene. Lanette had already graduated from California State Northridge University and was working for American Airlines by the time I joined the family. She found her adventure in life by traveling all over the world, including taking Granny and Papa on some of her international excursions. She married and birthed one daughter, Arika. She also opened a group home for girls, obtained a master's degree and settled into business management.

Approximately six months after becoming a part of the fabric of the Curry house and finding it to be a safe and secure environment, I received a startling call from Mom announcing she was moving to Palo Alto over the next week. She told me to return home to pack and move. Mom explained the purpose for the move was because her sister, Henrietta, was sick with cancer and she was going to go take care of her.

I was compassionate about my aunt's care and needs, but I was also concerned about my own care and needs. At this point, I had attended approximately ten schools and lived in twenty-three houses. I wanted the instability and insanity to end, but I didn't know how it would happen. Well, low and behold, Claudia came into my room to talk to me about whether I desired to leave or stay. I told her of course I wanted to stay, but I didn't know how it was going to happen. She insisted on going with me to speak with my mother.

When we arrived at Moms, Claudia took the lead. She talked to Mom about the possibility of me remaining here in Los Angeles with the Curry family while keeping the same arrangement we had been working with. Surprisingly, Mom was agreeable. So, I packed the rest of my stuff and headed off to live with the Curry's full time. From that day on, I was a full-blown member of the Curry clan. I actually for the first time had my own bedroom which had a bathroom in it to boot. I felt like I had hit the jackpot. I had love, shelter and a future ahead of me. God had delivered me as prophesied.

CHAPTER 17

Chance To Succeed

I headed to Crenshaw High School in fall of 1981 for my freshman year. It was pretty incredible to have a stable home life and having nothing in school to worry about except getting good grades. I also gained my first real job as an after-school teacher's assistant at K. Anthony Elementary. I loved my new life.

Then one night about half-way through the school year, Granny came into my bedroom. She came to speak with me about my plans for the future. She wanted to know if I wanted to go to college. I told her I did, and she shared they wanted to help me by saving money for that purpose. I told her that I was very grateful, and I thought my Dad sent child support. I wanted to call him to find out where it was going because it would be a big help for my college fund. After she left my room,

Courting with Chance

I telephoned my Dad. I assumed it would be an easy call.

In calling Dad, I gave him some background. I shared with him the circumstance of how I came to the Curry's and the plan they were now working on. Dad was very cautious. He paused and gave me a deliberate answer. He shared he had no idea I wasn't with Mom. Further, he stressed he paid child support because it was taken out of his check biweekly, but he had no idea where it was going. Lastly, he indicated he didn't want to deal with my mother because he had too much trouble with her and child support in the past.

After hanging up the phone, I immediately called Mom. I explained the situation to her and asked her if she knew where the child support was going. She replied she didn't know, but she would check on it and get back with me. I hung up the phone somewhat puzzled, but also with anticipation of getting to the bottom of the situation; naïve me. About two days later, I received a response, but it didn't come the way I anticipated.

Actually, the response came with a knock on the door by two police officers along with a social worker from the Child Protective Services (CPS). Apparently, Mom contacted the LAPD and reported I had been kidnapped and brainwashed by a family in Los Angeles. The social worker talked to me separately from the Curry's. She indicated because I wasn't related to the

Curry's, I couldn't legally live with them. She further informed us she would have to place me in foster care while she conducted her investigation, and she would be returning shortly. I was devastated and angry!

Every day thereafter, I waited and watched expecting the social worker to return.

Meanwhile, I endured threatening telephone calls from one of my brothers. It appeared Mom put him up to calling me to try and convince me to return home. When the "friendly, brotherly" calls didn't work, the threats began. Once the Curry's found out about the calls, they immediately put a stop to me receiving any calls from my brothers. At one point, even Hop seemed to agree with Mom that I should just pack up and move to Northern California to quash the big mess. But after Claudia had a talk with Hop about what the move might mean for my future, she acknowledged she had been misinformed and relented. Plus, by this time, Hop and Mathis had married, so she was completely away from Mom's influence.

In the interim, I was secretly dealing with another scary situation at church. The married choir director, Henry Hiderspin, began to make inappropriate moves toward me. The first couple of times it happened, I thought I was just conjuring up things in my imagination, but it wasn't long before he made his motives clear. Whenever we were alone in the back hallway, he blatantly kissed me. Again, I was still really confused about how to say no to men. But I knew what he was doing was wrong and not Christian like. I started making excuses about not wanting to go to church because I was too busy in school. Then one day, I walked out of school, right after the bell rang, and I was startled to see Henry parked in front of my school. It appeared he was looking for me, so I ran and hid. I never told the Curry's about him, but I made sure I was never alone with him ever again. I did have enough sense by then to realize I could keep myself out of harm's way by not giving opportunities to perpetrators, even at church.

Also, I worked as hard as I could in school because I really didn't know when my time with the Curry's would come to an end. Crenshaw High offered many school-based organizations, including MEDCOR, which was a program designed to encourage the study of math and science in preparation for a career in the medical field. At the time I participated in MEDCOR because I still thought I wanted to become a forensic pathologist. In addition to receiving tutoring at the University of Southern California on the weekends in math and science, during the summer we were promised a summer job at the Los Angeles County General Hospital. For my first summer job with MEDCOR, I worked in the Orthopedic Surgery unit. During this assignment, I recognized my dislike for blood, the hospital and morgue environment. I realized I would go stir crazy working in the morgue as much as I liked to talk because dead people do not talk back. Nevertheless, I still thought

I would explore becoming a different type of doctor because the medical field was all I had focused on.

Finally, we received a letter from the DPS indicating my case was set for a hearing. By this time, I had lived with the Curry's roughly two years and I felt more determined to keep my stability and defend their honor than I had in the beginning.

When the date arrived to go to court, I was ready. In addition to Granny and Papa, Claudia also joined us. I always felt an extra layer of security when Claudia was around. Once my case was called, the attorneys spoke first, and then I asked if I could speak to the judge. I told the judge I was grateful for him hearing my case and I recognized that he had a job to do. I further shared as much background as I could regarding the circumstances by which I came to live with the Curry's, and what they had done for me in the two years I lived with them. Also, I stressed I really needed the judge to know my mother was incapable of keeping me safe and secure. I shared I had an interest in attending college and I knew it would be nearly impossible, if I was returned to my mother. Finally, I told the judge if he had to remove me from the Curry's home and place me in foster care, I understood, and I would go wherever he placed me, but I implored him to give me a chance to succeed by not returning me to my mother's care.

Much to my amazement, the judge heard me and answered my plea. He terminated my mother's parental rights and placed me into the custody of the State of

California. In placing me in the custody of the State, I was placed into foster care. To my surprise, I found out the Curry's had obtained their foster care license over the previous two years we were waiting to go to court. So, I went back home with the Curry's and back to school at Crenshaw. The Curry's became my foster family.

The next summer I was presented with an awesome opportunity to attend the Junior Statesmen program at University California at Davis (UCD) near Sacramento. Once I found out I had been selected by my high school counselor, Ms. Washington, I was so excited. After Claudia met with Ms. Washington, all my plans were full steam ahead. I took my first airplane ride to UCD to attend the program. I arrived on campus and joined nearly one hundred other high school students from across the state. I still had the medical field at the forefront of my mind, but I enjoyed the challenge of the Junior Statesman's program focus on the government and engagement of my oral skills. The program was approximately eight weeks and we were allowed to reside in the college dorms. While there, Dad came to the campus to visit. He picked me up and took me to dinner. It was great seeing him, and he appeared to be happy seeing my small academic success in attending the UCD program. Upon the completion of the program, I returned to Los Angeles and headed into my senior year.

On my eighteenth birthday, I was scheduled to be emancipated from the foster care program effective upon graduation with plans to attend college at University of California at San Diego (UCSD). My whole world had changed unbelievably.

I gained an entirely new family with parents who didn't live in hostility toward each other, plus healthy relationships with my siblings. In addition, I had a new normal of buying new clothes for church events, driving Claudia and Lanette's sports' cars, traveling, celebrating everything from small academic accomplishments to work promotions and making Christmas lists. I was happily overwhelmed with the one hundred and eighty degree turn my life had taken. I was on top of the world and just looking forward to my twelfth-grade prom.

CHAPTER 18

Chance To Give Life

I decided I was going to be Cinderella for my prom because I had waited all my life to dress up in a ball gown. Claudia and Lanette made sure my outfit was perfect. Once I was asked to the prom by Cory, I was ready. Unfortunately, he had plans beyond the prom and I didn't have enough courage to resist his request. We spent our after-after prom at a local motel. Somehow in my naiveté I decided it was ok to have sex on prom night, because finally, I would be in total control of whom I shared my body, I thought. As I look back, I realize neither one of us really had a clue what we were doing. At least Cory had enough sense to bring a condom, even though it broke, and we continued having sex anyhow.

I'll never forget the very next day after returning

home from the prom, I was in Granny's closet doing something, when she looked at me and said, "You're pregnant, aren't you?" I quickly said, "No, what are you talking about?" Thinking I was busted, but it never crossed my mind that I might be pregnant. The following month I was shocked; Granny was right. I discovered I was pregnant when I decided to give blood to the Red Cross for a blood drive and fainted after the procedure. Upon going to the doctor to follow up on why I fainted, I took a pregnancy test and it came back positive.

For about one week, I didn't know what to do. I was already accepted into college and was gearing up for graduation in less than thirty days. Cory too had been accepted into a college. Neither of us was ready nor suitable to become parents. But, more than anything, I realized Cory was going to get his education regardless. It was me who had to decide what I would do. No matter what, I didn't want to end up like my mother. So, I decided to have an abortion. I didn't want my child relegated to a life of poverty especially since I only had a high school education. Also, I didn't know of any other options because I didn't dare tell Granny or Claudia. I was more afraid they would put moral pressure on me to keep the baby, and I didn't want them to feel any guilt for being responsible for my actions. So, two days before my high school graduation, I had an abortion. I had an overwhelming feeling of guiltand condemnation, including having a nightmare I died on the operating table.

After the abortion, I rested for a couple of hours and then went to buy shoes for graduation. It was at this time of reflection I realized just how selfish and impulsive I had been in aborting my baby. It was also at this moment I decided I would never have another abortion. Whatever happened from then on, I was willing to suffer the consequences because I no longer had any excuses. I knew the potential consequences I would be getting into by taking the risk of having unprotected sex outside of marriage which was against everything I learned in church.

Two days later, I graduated from high school with Papa, Granny, Claudia and Danielle from the Curry's. Also, from the Ackerson side: my cousin, Karen, Uncle Roy and Aunt Neda were in attendance. Following graduation, I went to grad night at Disneyland. Needless to say, it wasn't the happiest place on earth for me then.

CHAPTER 19

Life And Death Chances

I had one more task on my mind to accomplish the summer before I headed to college. I wanted to go visit Dad. I felt we had some unfinished business. I called him up and asked him about his plans for the upcoming weekend because I was headed to Sacramento. He said he was going to be out on the water fishing, and I could join him.

I took a plane to town with a plan of hearing Dad's perspective because pretty much all my life I had heard the stories of how no good Dad was courtesy of Mom of course. I heard more crazy things about my Dad than I had seen. But I also knew him as the Dad who inspired me because he use to send me $5 per "A" for my report card. I wanted to hear his side of the story. So, I used this opportunity for that purpose. I asked every question that ever entered my mind. I wanted to know what happened to cause the divorce.

Boy did I receive answers. Dad talked nonstop. He didn't seem to have an angry tone anymore, but he wanted to make sure I knew he was adamant about certain points. I realized I had to keep things in perspective too because I was actually now just getting his version, and later I would compare the two. Dad shared three shocking pieces of information: 1) At one time, before I was conceived, my older siblings were placed in foster care while under Mom's care and Dad kidnapped them and took them to Oklahoma, 2) Mom had been in a mental institution and 3) the background information on why Dad believed Hootnanne wasn't his child. Finally, I had one more question for Dad, "Are you sure you are my Daddy?" Then I added, "No pressure, because if you are not, I need to find him." Dad broke out in laughter. Then I looked at him and I started laughing. He then reassured me that he was my father.

After visiting with Dad, I made my way over to visit Mom. She was recuperating from an operation. Apparently while living in Palo Alto caring for Aunt Henrietta, Mom was attacked and stabbed with a knife by my Uncle Gus' estranged wife, Liza. Mom said Liza was angry because she believed Mom had butted into her marriage and talked against Liza to Uncle Gus. Mom said one day while she was waiting at a bus stop, Liza jumped out of a car, attacked and stabbed her in the stomach.

The stabbing was very violent and life threatening. Mom required surgery and a colostomy bag for her recovery.

I was able to go and visit with Mom while she recuperated. This was the first time I saw her since the entire legal action regarding her accusing the Curry's of kidnapping and brainwashing me. It was awkward between us, but we chatted, nevertheless. She apologized for how things turned out with me having to go to court, and she stated that if she couldn't raise me, she was glad the Curry's could. I accepted her apology and forgave her.

Unfortunately, things were also falling apart for Bolo and Hootnanne in Sacramento, too. They were suspected drug dealers and also accused of robbing a bank. The FBI came to Dad's house to question him. They asked Dad to view the surveillance picture and to see if he recognized anyone in the picture. Dad, true to form, said, "Nope, I don't recognize anyone in this picture. But, can I keep the picture?"

It seems the FBI did not have sufficient evidence to prosecute them on the bank robbery. Shortly thereafter, however, Hootnanne and Bolo ended up convicted of other crimes which landed them both in prison together, at the same time, in the same prison cell.

The month after I returned back home, I received a telephone call. Mutt had been injured in a vehicle accident in Sacramento. It wasn't a typical car accident.

Courting with Chance

He was working on his car placing an engine when the jack slipped causing him to be crushed underneath the car. Apparently, he lost oxygen for about twenty minutes and wasn't expected to live.

I packed my bags to go to Sacramento to join my family at Mutt's hospital bedside. I never once thought about the harm he caused me as a child. The only thing I could think about was my brother needed my prayers. Hop, Mathis and I arrived at the hospital to join Mom, Dig, Bull, and Mutt's wife, Anita. Mutt was hooked up to several machines, including life support.

I could feel a lot of tension between Mom, Dig and Anita. Hop and I tried our hardest to stay clear of the tension so we could focus on praying to keep Mutt alive. However, we still could feel the strife and conflict whenever Mom and Dig were in the room with Anita.

Hop, Mathis and I were preparing to head back to Los Angeles. Mom pulled us aside to announce she believed Anita was responsible for Mutt's condition. Mom accused Anita of kicking the jack which caused the car to crush Mutt.

Because Hop and I lived in Los Angeles, we hadn't had many interactions with Anita and were really unsure why Mom would accuse her of such horrific acts. Mom claimed Mutt was in the process of fixing his car so he could leave Anita, which was her motive. Mom also claimed to know individuals in Matthew's apartment complex who said they witnessed Anita kicking the jack and/or delaying the call to the paramedics.

About three months after we returned home, we received word Mutt had recuperated enough to be moved to a rehabilitation facility or home. Mom wanted him home with her, but Anita insisted he would be better served in a rehabilitation facility. Mutt was moved to a rehabilitation facility and he died that evening.

The story was told to us a little differently. Mom said that Mutt absolutely did not want to go to the rehabilitation facility, and he had in fact written a note saying that. Later, however, as I grappled with the fact that Mutt could not have written such a note with his desires on it, because I remembered he couldn't read or write. At the end of the day, I really considered Mutt's death as just an unfortunate incident especially since no criminal investigation ever took place. Yet, I also thought it was helpful in my personal healing process to not have to deal with him in my adult years.

CHAPTER 20

Redeeming Chance

I found great satisfaction, however, in loving, caring for and nurturing Mutt's son, Matthew Jr. He was five years old when Mutt died. He was being reared in Los Angeles by his mother, Tammy. She had four additional children after Mutt's death.

Matthew Jr. was my pride and joy. He was quick wit like my Dad and eager to learn like me. I worked really hard to keep in touch with Matthew Jr. and to keep him as safe as I could, even while I was with the Curry's. I picked him up once a week for dinner and took him to karate. When he heard the sound of my VW bug arriving, he would run to hide behind the big burly tree in front of his mother's apartment complex. He loved jumping from behind the tree to scare me. He was also very good in karate. His instructor said he could easily end up being a professional, if he could just get the discipline down.

I had a custom of giving Matthew Jr. his RTD bus fare a couple of weeks ahead of time to make sure he got to karate class, when I couldn't pick him up. I discovered that he missed a couple of karate practices and a lot of school. When I inquired, I found out why. I went straight over to Tammy's. Matthew Jr. answered the door. The house was a mess and all the children looked un-kept. Tammy was home but she was sleep. When I talked to Matthew Jr., I learned his mother hadn't bought food for the children, so he took his bus money to buy food and he remained home to care for his siblings. Unfortunately, crack cocaine had infiltrated our community, and Tammy was suspected of using it.

Also, it appeared Matthew Jr. was being scouted by the local street gangs. He had garnered a reputation for being fearless mostly because he had started defending his mother against the men who were coming to the house. After spending a couple of late afternoons accessing the situation, I realized Matthew Jr. had to be moved from that toxic environment to be saved from the streets of Los Angeles.

Matthew Jr. went to live with Tammy's aunt, Doris. Unfortunately, Matthew Jr. was steep in teenage mischievousness and slickness. Aunt Doris couldn't manage him much longer than about a year. We had to figure out another plan.

Courting with Chance

Aunt Doris and I spoke with Hop and Mathis about allowing Matthew Jr. to come to the Mojave Desert to live with them. After a couple of discussions, we packed Matthew Jr.'s bags and I took him to live with Mathis, Hop and their two girls: Annie and Dana. Then I turned my attention to attending UCSD.

CHAPTER 21

Chance To Fail Or Soar

Upon arriving at UCSD, I lived on campus my first year in a two-bedroom townhouse with a view of the water and bunked with three roommates: Vanessa Mealy, Roseland Jackson and Beverly Bianes. I was off to a great start just with the view alone at UCSD, but I quickly discovered the many schools and houses I grew up in were catching up with me academically. Although I entered college full of promise and passion, I was low on academic skill and self–discipline because I hadn't truly challenged myself once I returned to Los Angeles' schools from Hanford. Also, the freedom of college life and UCSD's proximity to Los Angeles' party scene, along with the parties on the military instillations in San Diego, was quite distracting.

I was now certain I no longer wanted to become a doctor. However, I wasn't sure of a new career path yet. I was going to class just enough to pass and going home on weekends to party with my close friend, Sharon. Alternatively, the partying consisted of me coordinating with my friends who were attending San Diego State University, so I could pick them up and head to the military base. We typically partied at the Devil Dog Inn Club located at the Navy Training Center (NTC). Our biggest concern and roadblock was we needed someone with a military identification (ID) in our car for entrance on the base. For that, we headed to the ARCO station down the street from NTC to accost one of the soldiers to escort us onto the base. Once we were in the club, we would lose our unsuspecting mule.

Partying was our only past time. Even so, I knew I had to keep my wits about me to make sure nothing went wrong in the risky situations we were flirting with, so I was always the designated driver. Being the designated driver meant I had to refrain from drinking alcohol because I needed to make sure we all returned home safely. During this period, I became hooked on Shirley Temples, a non-alcoholic drink, because they taste good and look grown-up. As cautious as I was trying to be, one particular night, I made a bad judgment call and almost paid dearly with my life.

Monique, my old neighbor, was attending nearby San Diego State, so we partied together. One particular Saturday, we partied all day and into the night with guys from Camp Pendleton Marine Base. After attending several parties, and realizing it was about two o'clock in the morning, we agreed to give the guys a lift back to the base. After leaving the base to head back to campus, I let Monique drive because I had promised to teach her how to drive a stick shift. We pulled over and traded seats. She was driving just a little faster than the speed limit, but it really didn't matter because the freeway was pretty scarce at that time of morning. Just as the 5 and 805 freeways split heading back to San Diego, I told Monique to go toward the 5, but she thought she heard 805, thus when she realized her error, she over-corrected. At that moment, the car veered straight for the cliff to my right. All I could do was yell, "JESUS!" and pull the emergency brake. The car spun around and came to a complete stop in the opposite direction. As we stopped screaming and looked up, we could see headlights from the cars of oncoming traffic facing us. The cars heading our way had come to a stop about fifty feet back. It was as if they had been stopped so they wouldn't collide with us. Whew!!! It was only a miracle we were still alive. I decided thereafter to use the name of Jesus for any crisis I encountered, because it worked. I also noted I had made a misjudgment which could've cost us our lives in letting Monique drive. Even though I hadn't been drinking, I forgot Monique had. Had we crashed the headlines would've read: "Two college students dead in an alcohol related accident." Boy was I glad when I finished my first year, even though I was on academic probation. I was just glad to be alive.

Courting with Chance

By the second year, the Curry's were so proud of me they purchased a townhouse off campus for me to share with my niece, Kim, Hazel's daughter. Kim was a year ahead of me attending San Diego State. The Curry's had no idea I was on academic probation.

Upon my return to campus, I decided to visit the financial aid office for guidance considering my probationary status. While speaking with the financial aid advisor, she excused herself to leave the room to go obtain information for me. When she stepped away, I noticed the paperwork on her desk had one of my roommate's name on it, Vanessa Mealy. The document was a request to leave school for the purpose of enlisting in the US Navy Reserves. I had never heard of the military Reserves, but I was curious now.

I left the financial aid office and headed to the career center to find more answers because I knew I wasn't focused. At the career center I took a battery of tests which considered my personality, values, and interests. The results all pointed to law enforcement. I considered the FBI or CIA, but I just didn't see myself doing either because I wasn't interested in carrying a gun or living in secret. Continuing my research, I stumbled upon the Air Force (AF) Reserves. I decided to join the AF Reserves because I wanted my own ID to get on the military base to party. Also, I needed to get away from everyone to make my own decision about the direction of my future.

Convincing the Curry's of my plan to go to the AF Reserves was the most difficult of all. It seemed they had developed a sour taste in their mouths for the military because of my brother, James' Vietnam experience. They gave me much consternation, thinking my college goals and career dreams would be derailed if I enlisted in the military. Claudia was particularly critical and discouraged it. By this time, Claudia's approval was so significant to me. I'm not even sure how or why I continued considering joining the military after her reaction, except I knew I had to go to the military to get away from everyone to make my own decisions.

Monique also took the AF entrance exam with me and she scored very high making her eligible for more money. We had hopes of joining the AF Reserves on the buddy program, however those hopes were dashed when she failed to show up for the swearing-in. She told me she couldn't bring herself to leave knowing her boyfriend, Paul, was returning from Westpac as part of his Navy duty. I forged ahead anyway.

I admit my priorities were mixed up in seeking after a military career for the ID card to get on the base to go party. However, once I stepped foot on Lackland AF Base (AFB) in San Antonio, Texas for boot camp, I realized my plight was much bigger than my plan. Being introduced to the huge bugs and extreme heat in Texas was my focus in my initial letters home to the Curry's, Sharon and anyone else who would listen. Once I settled in, boot camp was empowering, hard, enlightening, conforming and plain old fun. Being woken up every morning, at the crack of dawn, to the loud sound of "REVEILLE, REVEILLE, RISE AND SHINE," is jarring, but calming over time. Lining up in formation to march over for breakfast and then physical training (PT) was how we started each day. Every morning I ran the required distance in PT with the help of my favorite Bible scripture back then: "I can do all things through Christ which strengthens me." Philippians 4:13.

I figured out immediately the role of the Technical Instructor (TI). My TI was there to be in my face to take me all the way to my limit and find out my breaking point. No matter how crazy the insults sounded, I realized they were directed at my behavior, not my spirit. Once I came to this realization, it was smooth sailing. Thereafter, I just viewed my experience as an opportunity to learn more about myself and meet new people from different parts of the country with different cultures and various levels of education. I actually began to appreciate the lessons learned in all the moving I endured as a child.

I successfully completed basic training in Texas and technical school at Keesler AFB in Biloxi, Mississippi, including enduring a Hurricane. Whew! I returned home and re-entered UCSD as a junior, as I promised the Curry's. I changed my major to sociology and minor to prelaw. Immediately I noticed a difference in my passion for learning. One of my favorite classes was a literature class. In addition to enjoying the subject matter, I had a very supportive Caucasian professor. She counseled me regarding my writing deficiencies and also stressed that I would be a force to reckon with, and a leader of my people, once I learned to clearly convey my thoughts in written form.

As for my military commitment, I continued to serve in the AF Reserves one weekend per month and two weeks out of the year, which was typically during the summer. In the AF Reserves, originally, I was a safety administrator, which is basically a glorified secretary. After getting a grip on my goals, and specifically considering the law, I cross-trained into the legal specialist field. Then, I returned to technical school at Keesler AFB to attend the paralegal specialist program the following summer.

Upon returning home a second time, Claudia offered me an internship at her law office. I gladly accepted. Claudia was focusing on probates, family law and personal injury cases. It seemed I was finally finding my way now that I was focusing on the law. Plus, interning at my sister's law firm was intriguing and empowering because I yielded far more power than I should have been given. Yet, being in that environment made me realize I could use my voice to help the needy. Claudia often shared that she thought I would be a good criminal defense attorney. I didn't think so because I secretly believed that I would just end up representing my brothers. I had no interest in that prospect.

For my AF Reserve duty, my work assignment changed to the Judge Advocate General's (JAG) office. I really enjoyed my new assignment because I was working with attorneys on active cases. The attorneys were officers and all other support staff, including the paralegals, were enlisted. There were just a couple of problems. I recognized right away the paralegals did the lion's share of the work. Doing all the leg work and having to also salute the officers, was enough for me to realize I had to change my game plan. I decided then to become an attorney. So, I returned to UCSD in order to graduate in preparation for acceptance into law school.

My graduation from UCSD in 1987 was a proud moment for both of my families. Most of the Curry's attended my graduation along with Mom, Hop, Uncle Roy and Aunt Neda on the Ackerson side. It was a warm and exciting day in San Diego. As I marched with my graduating class through the cheering crowd, I looked out from the bleachers into the crowd of family and friends. I was happy to see everyone, but especially surprised to see my Mom. Next to Mom, I spotted my sister, Hop, holding up a fur coat. She was pointing at Mom and me yelling, "It's for you!" Apparently, Mom had brought me a fur coat as my graduation gift. It was funny to me because in that instance I felt like I was in a 1970s episode of "The Beverly Hillbillies." I was also conflicted because I wandered whether Mom was trying to use that gift thinking she had to compete with the Curry's. The Curry's, on the other hand, were gracious.

After graduation, I decided to work full time in the AF Reserves for one year in order to further solidify my interest in the law and enhance my law school application. I knew I would have difficulty on the Law School Achievement Test (LSAT). I was always a horrible standardized test taker. So, I needed to bring other qualities to the law school table. Also, there was a shortage of paralegals, which meant I received many opportunities to travel that year. In addition to being stationed at March AFB, Riverside, California, I also traveled to Washington State, Arizona and Europe to relieve paralegals. I had a great military learning experience and a wonderful life experience. During that year, I took the LSAT and scored low, as anticipated. I still applied for law school. I was accepted into Whittier College School of Law in its Summer Performance Program. The promise was, if I successfully completed the Summer Performance Program, I would be admitted into the fall class. I did both.

To supplement my income once I started my first year of law school, in addition to the AF Reserves, I also worked a graveyard shift at a group home for delinquent and neglected girls called Penny Lane in Van Nuys, California.

While away in Europe for my reserve duty, Penny Lane hired a young lady, Bernadette Harris, to substitute in my absence. Upon my return from Europe, Bernadette indicated the girls talked non-stop about how strict I was, and she was excited to meet me, since the girls spent so much time comparing us. Bernadette and I became fast friends. So much so that Bernadette invited me to join her family on a trip to the United States Supreme Court (The Supreme Court). Her mother had been the victim of police brutality in Ohio and the lawsuit filed by her family reached the steps of The Supreme Court. Wow, I was honored and blown away just to think about the possibility, and I didn't hesitate to say yes. Claudia and the Curry family knew how important this opportunity was, so they were very supportive in making sure I attended the event.   I flew to Washington, D.C. in the winter of 1988 to observe oral arguments in the case known as *Harris v. City of Canton Ohio, 489 U.S. 378 (1989)*.

Arriving on the steps of The Supreme Court is magical for a first-year law student. In addition, having the opportunity to somehow be connected to one of the cases before the Court, no matter how tangential, is awesome too. And, in this case, having the opportunity to see history play out with individuals like Justice Thurgood Marshall and Chief Justice Rehnquist was thrilling. But I also obtained another benefit. Bernadette's middle sister, Emanuella Groves, was a practicing attorney at the time. She participated in an admission's ceremony where she was sworn-in to argue before The Supreme Court just before oral arguments. Observing the ceremony was life changing for me! I remember thinking one day I would like to do the same, but I knew it meant I had to successfully complete law school and pass the California Bar. So, I just tucked that experience back into the crevices of my mind and heart.

While in law school, my writing deficiencies began to show up again. One of my classmates, Beth Belzer, miraculously came to my rescue. Beth was a very wealthy, mature student who confessed she only came to law school to figure out how to protect herself legally in her divorce battle with her physician ex-husband. Beth had successfully raised two sons who were also physicians and she saw law school as a place to get just enough knowledge to intelligently help herself. Upon Beth learning I was having difficulties with my writing skills, she unilaterally recruited her daughter-in-law, Nina, who was an English professor at the local university, to assist me. Thereafter, I spent several weekends meeting with Nina, learning the rules of English. Upon completion, I found my confidence in writing. Shortly thereafter, I entered a Moot Court competition wherein I needed to submit a written brief and present oral argument. Since Nina was out of the country, I was on my own for writing and editing the written brief. I was so excited when I received word, I landed a spot on Whittier's Moot Court Team. This meant I had finally learned the rules of English, followed them, and successfully accomplished my goal.

In addition to my AF Reserve duty and Penny Lane, I also rejoined Claudia's staff as a paralegal. Claudia had married, and she shared office space with her husband, Dirk Streets. He operated a real estate and tax company. Dirk gave the three companies the name Streets Business Services (SBS). This encompassed the law firm, real estate and a tax company. Oddly enough, he represented himself as the CEO of all three, even though only an attorney can legally own a law firm.

While working at SBS, I started dating one of the law firm's clients, Austin Brazille.

As the paralegal, I pretty much ran the law firm in Claudia's absence, which was very exciting and enticing, yet I was aware of my own inadequacies. Claudia was use to flying by the seat of her pants and doing really well at it. I was not good at it due to my ridged military training, so I decided to seek out more formal training.

I applied for a law clerk position with the Los Angeles City Attorney's Office at the Airport Division. I was hired.

Like the military, the City Attorney's Office was a night and day experience from SBS. I worked with nine assistant city attorneys and one supervising paralegal, Michelle Anderson. Our job was to represent the City against any claims related to the Los Angeles Airport. Additionally, I gained a new mentor, Sheryl Meshack, an incredible litigator who was authentic, personable and very funny. Although Sheryl was my favorite attorney there, I still made it my business to volunteer for assignments with the other attorneys because I knew I wanted a broader experience, and I didn't want to make any enemies.

CHAPTER 22

Defying Chance

During my last year of law school, I had an interesting question asked of me while I was in the student lodge waiting for class to begin. A couple of my classmates were having a conversation about the California State Bar. One of them attempted to bring me into the conversation using sarcasm. He said, "Karen, Whittier has a very low bar passage rate, what are you going to do?" I looked at him with a puzzled expression and said, "What do you mean what am I going to do? Actually, statistics do not control my life because if they did, I wouldn't be here with you in law school. I am here because I'm the exception to the rule. By the way, is there a 1% passage rate? Because that is all I need, right?" He really didn't know how to respond, and I didn't expect him to. I have absolutely no idea how things turned out for that young man. I do know that that conversation gave me one more reason to study hard and pass the California Bar the first time.

I graduated law school the same month my enlistment was up in the AF Reserves, May 1991. I was grateful to have the luxury of studying for the Bar uninterrupted because of financial support from my boyfriend, Austin, and the family support of the Curry's. Upon passing the Bar the first time, I instinctively knew I owed the praise to Jesus. Considering my childhood roadblocks and my test taking history, I knew God's miraculous hand and His timing were all in my favor. I also knew my success was due to having the benefit of shadowing Claudia during her study for the Bar several years before.

First, I thought it would be perfect to stay on with the City Attorney's Office as a Deputy City Attorney. But the City Attorney's Office had a freeze on for hiring deputies. Thus, I was told only one of us paralegals from the Airport Division was going to be hired as a Deputy City Attorney. Michelle had the most seniority, so she was promoted to the position. I was disappointed that they could only promote one of us, but I decided to forge ahead.

I considered returning to SBS. However, by this time, the implosion of SBS had taken place, so it wasn't an option.

Also, in my love life things were falling apart.

Courting with Chance

Austin and I had become engaged, but we broke up because he said he loved me but was not in love with me anymore. I knew this was the oldest excuse in the relationship book, which was code for being unfaithful. Fortunately, my longtime friend, Monique, encouraged me to join her on a "no holds bar" trip to Bermuda.

Upon arriving in Bermuda, once we got settled into our hotel, we rented a moped to get around the island. Apparently, a moped and taxi were the only transportation for non-residents on the island. After a fifteen-minute moped lesson, I decided to drive, and Monique agreed to be the backseat navigator. As we approached the main intersection on the island, Monique got confused on her directions and simultaneously I could not find the moped brakes. Within seconds we realized we were in trouble when we found ourselves careening across the intersection, airborne, and ultimately crashing into the back of a parked car. After getting over the shock of the crash, and as we were getting our bearings, we looked and saw a woman running toward us and yelling, "Call the police, the Americans hit my car!" Fortunately, we had insurance and the police resolved the matter quickly.

Sitting on the curbside and taking a deep breath, we decided to head to the beach. At our next stop at the beach, we saw a gentleman in a full-body cast. Upon chatting with him and his wife, we discovered that he had been injured in a moped accident. Monique and

I just looked at one another and shook our heads. We realized how blessed we were to still be in one piece. We ordered a drink and enjoyed the rest of our vacation without a glitch.

I returned home charged and ready to move on with my life. I put the word out with my friends that I was seeking an entry level attorney position. I accepted legal contract work with local law firms to keep my bills paid. One was at Ernest & Sams. I met with Craig Ernest and he agreed to hire me for a bargain basement monthly salary in exchange for training and experience I yearned for. I started work at Ernest & Sams as an associate and right away I was given a caseload, which included defending corporate clients. It was really exciting having the feeling of joining a prestigious law firm. In addition, Craig had a really great partner, Leslie Sams. Leslie was very smart, deliberate and trustworthy, even from the start. Early on, I got the impression Craig was the business mind and Leslie was the legal mind. I discovered this impression was accurate. Unfortunately, on a couple of occasions I also witnessed Craig using profanity at the office manager. I simply made a mental note that I wouldn't take that kind of mistreatment because I had studied and gone to school far too long to be subjected to such behavior.

I sometimes found myself asking Craig to review my assignments because I wanted to make sure I was on the right track. He seemed to be low on extra time

133

for training back then, but high on time for showing off the firm. So, it wasn't unusual for Craig to give guided tours around the firm, especially for women.

During this period, I lived alone in a one-bedroom rear duplex on Van Ness Avenue near Florence Avenue in Los Angeles. One night, I was sound asleep when I had a nightmare. I felt like I was leaving my body and being chased by a fury, ugly, miniature creature I believed was a demon. As I left my body, I was running, but not on the ground, I was being chased in the air around the ceiling of my apartment by the demon. The demon was holding a weapon, but I couldn't quite figure out what it was at first. After running all around the small apartment, I ran back into my body to escape the creature. As I returned to my body, the creature tried to pin me down. It was then I realized the creature had a long butcher knife in its hand and it was using the knife to try to pierce my chest. Just as I saw the first strike come toward my chest, I yelled, "Jesus!" As I yelled "Jesus," the creature fell back. Then he tried to come toward me again, and I yelled "Jesus" again. At that point, because the creature flew backwards again, I realized the name of Jesus was working. So, I just began to say Jesus! Jesus! Jesus! The next thing I knew, I was coming out of the nightmare and panting as I opened my eyes. It felt so real!

After this horrific nightmare, I prayed for the meaning of it. The only thing I heard in my spirit was the enemy was trying to use the tool of sex to kill my spirit. At the time, I didn't have a clue of what that meant, but I realized my childhood of sexual victimizations was probably a part of the big picture.

Then, about two weeks later, I returned home from work and noticed my back-door security gate was broken. I just thought I would bring it to my landlord's attention and have it fixed over the next couple of days. That night, my teenage nephew, Matthew Jr. was visiting from the Mojave Desert. At about two o'clock in the morning, he ran into my bedroom to tell me he heard a loud thump on the back door. After gathering my senses, I too heard someone trying to kick in my back door. I picked up the phone to call 911 and went to grab a twenty-two-caliber pistol that Austin had left at my house because I lived in a bad neighborhood. As Matthew Jr. was talking to the 911 operator, I yelled to tell the intruder he better not come through the door because if he did, I would shoot him. Simultaneously, I realized I had to use the bathroom because my stomach was in knots. I turned to my nephew to give him the gun, so I could go to the bathroom. As I turned to Matthew Jr., he was standing in a ready position like Rambo with a butcher knife and rubbing alcohol in his hand. I knew the intruder was going to be handled one way or another, if he came through the door.

Soon after calling 911, the police arrived to find a deranged, intoxicated, naked man at my back door.

Courting with Chance

I looked out my door once the police handcuffed him, and recognized the intruder was one of my landlord's handymen. He had actually rigged the back door so it wouldn't close because he said he had a plan to come and rape me. But God had another plan, praise God!

Back at work, I was assigned to work on a federal case. I felt completely overwhelmed and untrained to work independently on that type of case, but I forged ahead awaiting Craig's input.

Earlier on the same day, my girlfriend from the Supreme Court, Bernadette, stopped by the firm to bring me something. Also, this just happened to be the day the Rodney King verdicts were anticipated in Simi Valley. The Rodney King case was about a black motorist who attempted to evade the police and upon his capture, he was beaten by white officers. Because the beating was videotaped, there was a high expectation the white officers would be punished criminally for their actions. However, as the staff took a short break in our workload to watch the televised verdicts, the mood quickly changed to somber when all of the white officers were found not guilty. Considering I had lots of work waiting for me, I couldn't dwell on that. I went back to the grind. At some point in the late afternoon, I received a call from my paralegal, Bobby, who had left earlier that day. Bobby was calling to tell me to wrap up my work and get home early because it looked like a riot was brewing in my neighborhood.

He said, "Karen, you need to get home before night fall. You're not that dark and you're riding in a black car with tinted windows. You might get yanked from your car!" I heard Bobby, but I also continued to work because I couldn't imagine anyone would actually be pulled out of their car.

While wrapping things up, I went into the copy room to make some copies. Craig came in shortly after me. In our effort to ignore the obvious outside, we started with small talk. Somehow Craig and I began to talk about the trophies (women he liked). I mentioned I knew the type of women he liked, and I could point them out in a crowd. He responded, "I think otherwise, like your girlfriend who was in the office earlier today (Bernadette), she's okay, but she's not stopping traffic." Before thinking, I shot back, "Well, you're not causing any accidents yourself!" As the words left my mouth and I observed Craig's face, I realized I had made an unforgivable mistake. I could feel my mouth had gotten me in trouble again, but it was too late because I couldn't un-ring the bell. I quickly gathered my papers and excused myself.

I lived within a mile of the riot's hotspot at the intersection of Florence Avenue and Normandie Avenue, so I was just glad to make it home before nightfall. My entire neighborhood seemed to be burning down. Blackness, ash, sirens and chaos was everywhere. I was horrified to see the news coverage of the truck driver and others pulled from their vehicles on Florence and Normandie. I couldn't help but think about Bobby's warning earlier that day.

The next morning, after a long restless night, I heard the telephone ring. My new roommate, Randy, came to my door to hand me the phone, and he told me the caller identified himself as my boss. I answered the phone saying, "Hello." Craig inquired as to who answered my phone. I was so out done by his question because I thought it was none of his business, so I said, "Craig, the last time I checked, I come to work and do my work so you can give me a paycheck. With my paycheck, I pay Pacific Bell, not you. So, you have no right to know who answered my phone! How can I help you otherwise?" He simply blurted out, "I'm calling because I know you live in the riot area and I was planning to tell you to stay home, but now I am ordering you to bring your black ass to work!"

I hung up the phone shaking my head in disgust, but I proceeded to get dressed for work. As I got dressed, I realized things were completely haywire outside of my house and the surrounding areas. I didn't know what I would be faced with. I decided to take Austin's gun with me just in case I faced violence. So, I put the pistol in my brief case and left for work. Arriving downtown, it appeared most offices were closed, but not Ernest & Sams.

Upon entering the firm, I could read the face of the receptionist. She appeared very nervous and she directed me to go to speak directly with Mr. Ernest, so I headed to Craig's office. Once I saw him, he immediately began to criticize the legal work I had done the day before. He complained about the fact that I was constantly saying I wanted more training. He said he was going to fix my problem. He told me to go down to my office and he would be there shortly. I complied. Upon entering my office, I saw the legal work on my desk with marks on it. I sat down at my desk and proceeded to address the corrections. Craig entered my office without knocking, and indicated he wanted me to move my office down the hall to the secretarial port just outside of his office so I could obtain the oversight I was seeking. I told him I didn't have a problem with his request, but I wanted to get the discovery corrected first. He stood near my door, slammed it and yelled, "You're going to move your office now, god dammit!" I was so shocked and furious at his behavior. I took one second, looked up at him from my desk and took a deep breath. In an instant, I was seeing red! I also considered there was a riot going on outside, I had a gun in my briefcase, and it was the wrong time of the month for me. I stood up and reached for my pager which was on my hip. Craig looked at me and said, "Oh, are you quitting?!" In a quiet, but solemn voice, I responded, "Yes, for your sake." I placed my pager on the desk, grabbed my purse and briefcase, and walked out.

Courting with Chance

When I arrived at the elevator, Leslie was standing there. She saw my face and said, "Damn, he always does this to the good ones!" The elevator doors opened, Leslie and I entered together. We decided to go grab a bite to eat. We ended up in Marina Del Rey, had lunch and headed back to Los Angeles, but we were stalled when I realized my gas tank was empty, and all the gas stations had closed because of fear of rioters. It was a long evening.

I woke up the next day with the realization of no longer having a job. Things were still hectic from the aftermath of the riot, so I knew I needed to wait a couple of days before I did anything. The beginning of the following week, as I cast my net out, I quickly noticed all the smaller law firms I interviewed with felt similar to the environment I had just left.

Then, one day I was approached by Jim, my sister, Claudia's friend. Jim worked in his brother's law office in the same suite of law offices Claudia had previously rented. Jim inquired if I was interested in opening my own law firm because his brother was selling his law firm. I told him absolutely not because I needed stability and benefits. He encouraged me to consider the fact that I could always go work for someone else, but I wouldn't always have an opportunity to work for myself. I told him I didn't have the resources for such a venture, but Jim was persistent. I paid the brothers eighteen hundred dollars from my tax refund to purchase the office furniture including copy machine, books, telephones, and client list. I taped my name on the door and opened for business the next day as the Law Offices of Karen M. Ackerson.

Then, just about two weeks after the riots occurred, I was watching television and breaking news came on. The LAPD was looking for at least eight gang members who were allegedly responsible for the eruption of the violence at the intersection of Florence and Normandie which sparked the riots. Specifically, they were seeking individuals who drug motorist Reginald Denny from his truck and beat him, as well as many other victims.

As I watched, I spotted Henry Keith Watson aka Keke. Keke was a neighbor and god-brother to my cousin, Karen, a childhood friend of mine and someone I had previously dated in my youth. I knew him to be a former US Marine and married with two daughters, so watching the news story was perplexing to me. I immediately picked up the phone and called his sister, Penny, my hair stylist. Penny shared, Keke had just been arrested and her family was in shambles as a result. Penny also indicated her parents already called in an attorney, Earl Broady, Jr., to defend Keke, but Keke was being very difficult because of all the high emotions charged from the Rodney King jury decision which he felt was unjust. Keke would not even talk to Earl. I inquired of Penny if she thought I could help and let her know I was available if they needed me. A couple of days later, I received a call from Penny asking if I would at least try to talk to Keke to get him to open up to Earl. I agreed and planned a trip to Wayside Correctional Facility, which is where Keke was detained.

Upon my arrival at Wayside, I was escorted to the attorney/client room to see Keke arrive handcuffed and shackled while escorted by several sheriff deputies with a video camera. Keke appeared to have been treated well considering his plight. He also seemed to give a sigh of relief to know I was helping smooth things over between him and Earl. After visiting for about an hour, I left and told him I would return. From that point on, I worked side by side with Earl. I volunteered originally because I recognized the great learning possibilities, but I clearly had no clue or insight of the possible risk.

Originally, there were about eight men charged in the Reginald Denny case, but the case first dwindled down to four main defendants. The most culpable was Damion Williams, who was known as Football Williams. He was accused of hitting Reginald Denny with a brick, with an action reminiscent of a football touchdown move. Keke was viewed as the second most culpable because he was the person who allegedly assaulted Reginald Denny by placing his foot on his neck. The other two men were even less culpable.

In preparation for the preliminary hearing, Earl was totally selfless, truly allowing me to help wherever I could. Although this was only my second preliminary hearing, I was quite confident because I felt I had a great security blanket in Earl Broady, Edi Faal, Wilma Shanks and other seasoned litigators on the case representing other defendants. My hunch was right. I couldn't have paid for the extensive experience I gleaned.

A couple of weeks later, while the Reginald Denny pretrial matters were proceeding, I received my first solo criminal case, *People v. Alondra Burke.* Ms. Burke was charged with aggravated mayhem and assault because of a domestic violence dispute between her and her daughter's father. Apparently, a fight ensued between the two when the child's father failed to return their child to Ms. Burke after a visit. Ms. Burke reported to the police she worried all night before the child was returned home the next evening. Upon returning the child, the father became outraged when confronted with his actions and she informed him that his visits would be stopped. He allegedly pulled out a razor blade and my client claimed she accidentally cut him across the face while defending herself. The scar across the victim's face was long and deep.

Ms. Burke was very nice and unassuming, appearing to only have the best interest of her child at heart. She and her roommate, Rita, relayed the story and were adamant of Ms. Burke's innocence. Nothing in the story was inconsistent, so I forged ahead with my self-defense theory. Since this trial was proceeding while I was also working on the Reginald Denny case, I was really learning as I went.

On the day of the Burke trial, I arrived at the courthouse early to get rid of my first-time jitters. Bernadette also came as moral support. The prosecution called their first witness, which was the victim. He seemed to testify pretty consistently with what I expected from the discovery. We took a break after the victim's direct examination and before returning for cross examination, Bernadette informed me that the victim had spoken to her in the hallway. He had changed his story. I informed the prosecution and the judge of this new information. I was able to cross examine the victim on this new evidence and add Bernadette to my witness list.

The prosecution rested after calling a couple of the emergency personnel who responded to the 911 call and the investigating officer.

In my defense case, I called my first witness, Ms. Burke's roommate, Rita. It wasn't until Rita walked by the counsel table and headed to the witness stand, in front of the jury box, that I got an epiphany. It was at that fleeting moment when I looked at the way the jurors were looking at Rita that I suspected that Rita and my client were also lovers. Rita, Bernadette and Ms. Burke testified. We rested and it was all up to the jury at this point. I was in deep prayer and reflection just knowing a conviction for aggravated mayhem carried a life sentence.

The jurors returned with a verdict. Ms. Burke was found not guilty of aggravated mayhem, but guilty of simple mayhem. It was bittersweet. I was elated Ms. Burke wouldn't spend the rest of her life in prison but terrified she would be separated from her child for any length of time based on what I believed happened. It was such a burden. I waited until the jurors left the courtroom and I cried. We concluded the hearing and set a sentencing date.

I returned to court with a motion to set aside the verdict, which fell on deaf ears, and then I proceeded to prepare for the approaching sentencing. In preparation, I met with Ms. Burke a couple more times. She knew prison time was likely given the judge's reaction to the post-trial motion, but of course it was my goal to find mitigating circumstances to keep the incarceration to a minimum.

One night after our final meeting, I headed home. As I was nearing my house, I did what I always do, I scoped out the scenery to ensure I was safe. As I took a quick look around, I spotted a familiar face in a car near my house. As I looked closer without alerting the person, I recognized the person sitting in the car was Rita, Ms. Burke's roommate. I was dumbfounded. I thought, "Why is this woman outside of my house?"

Courting with Chance

I entered my driveway and headed to the back of my duplex as I normally did, this time making haste to enter my back door. As soon as I entered my apartment, I headed to my telephone and called Ms. Burke to find out why Rita was outside of my house. When I reached Ms. Burke, she was totally apologetic. She explained Rita was there because Ms. Burke told Rita she was in love with me. Consequently, because Ms. Burke had requested Rita not attend the two post trial meetings, Rita assumed Ms. Burke and I were having an affair. (Apparently Rita repossessed cars for a living and used her work resources to find my house.) Again, I was totally dumbfounded.

I made it my business to be as nice as I could, and as clear as I could in conveying my position. I shared with Ms. Burke everything I had ever done for her was purely intended to be as her legal representative and nothing more. I further shared that I only had eyes for men. Finally, I asked her to please communicate clearly with Rita, nothing other than business had ever and would ever transpire between us. She did and Rita went away.

Ms. Burke was subsequently sentenced to one year in state prison. This first trial made it clear; I should not be personally invested in any criminal case. I learned it would always be difficult to get the full truth from people fighting for their lives, livelihood or reputation.

However, I was already committed to helping my childhood friend, Keke, and after finishing *People v. Burke*, the Reginald Denny trial was ready to begin. By the time the actual trial date arrived, the two less culpable defendants were severed from the case, so Keke and Damian Williams were standing trial together.

Since I had participated in the preliminary hearing, I had a great working knowledge of the expected testimony or the trial. Specifically, I was aware the prosecution had an uphill battle with proving premeditation because of the spontaneous eruption of violence. We hired an expert to testify about the mob violence mentality. Over the next year, we recognized this simple strategy was a huge key to a successful outcome. After a discussion with Earl, he permitted me to present the opening statement on behalf of Keke. Although this was one of the first trials televised from beginning to end, I didn't back down from the opportunity to play a major role in the case because I knew the evidence since I participated in the preliminary hearing. Our plan was to show the violence was not orchestrated thus negating premeditation. I felt totally confident about our plan because I had the words of the witnesses in my hands (transcripts).

The district attorney's office offered a plea bargain of seventeen years state prison. Keke rejected the offer. I was relieved because I believed that the evidence didn't support their offer and I didn't want a reputation in the community of selling my client out.

Courting with Chance

Televising the trial took the proceedings to a new level, including resulting in my own fifteen minutes of fame. It allowed for new friends and caused old friends to resurface, including my ex-fiancé, Austin.

Near the end of the trial, I discovered I was pregnant. I was unmarried and at the beginning of my legal career. Some people thought having a baby then might threaten my career, but I knew I had a promise to keep to myself and God. I didn't have a second thought. I was keeping my baby.

Around this same time, Earl requested permission to be excused from the trial to participate in a hunting trip he participated in biannually. After a brief discussion, which included the judge inquiring as to my presence and willingness to take the verdicts in Earl's absence, he was excused. It wasn't until the jury verdicts were being read; not guilty, not guilty, not guilty, guilty, hung, that I realized the magnitude of the case.

That evening, Keke was released with a time-served sentence on the simple assault charge he was found guilty of because he had already served seventeen months awaiting trial. Damion Williams was sentenced to eight years in state prison on an assault with a deadly weapon (the brick) conviction. Since Keke was released and Earl was still away hunting, the media wanted to hear from Keke, so I became the solo voice for our defense team. Gaining experiences on news outlets like

BET, CNN, World News, and Phil Donahue Show was enlightening, gratifying and humbling all at the same time. Also, after this trial, I had won the confidence and credibility of my community without ever paying a dime for advertisement. However, everyone wasn't excited about the seemingly slap on the hand for my client. As a matter of fact, I received several death threats. So much so, I moved out of my apartment and moved into Austin's house as a safety measure.

CHAPTER 23

Chance To Change Direction

I decided not to get caught up in the media hype, but rather to just quietly return to my private practice while I prepared for my baby's birth.

My practice consisted of criminal defense, civil rights' prosecution and personal injury cases. One day, while appearing in the Inglewood Juvenile Court where I was on the juvenile panel, I went down into the basement to visit my juvenile clients. I started a conversation with one of the public defenders, a young Jewish lady. She asked me, "What are you doing down here?" I responded, "What do you mean? I have a bar card like you. I'm here to see my client." She looked very perplexed when she said, "Oh no, I mean because you're pregnant. My boss is pregnant, and she obtained a waiver, so she doesn't have to come down here because it could be dangerous." I was so embarrassed

I had responded to her with such a chip on my shoulder. I apologized and followed her suggestion.

One day while I was walking the halls of the same court and conferring with my clients, I was approached by a middle-aged black man. He said, "Hi, can I get your help? I'm Bobby Womack and I'm here with my son who they say was a part of a robbery. They said he had a gun, but I don't believe he did it. I don't know when they are going to call his case, but I need to get out of here and go to the studio. Is there any way you can find out when they'll call his case?"

As a child, because Mom loved the blues and worked for several entertainers, I had been exposed to the music of many, including blues and R& B singer, Bobby Womack. But, because of my experience with Riser and James, I was not star struck. I told Mr. Womack to have a seat and I would at least find out who his son's attorney was so he would know who he should speak with about his scheduling issues. I did what I promised and went on about my business.

On January 17, 1994, the Northridge earthquake hit mightily in the San Fernando Valley and around Los Angeles. Lots of lives were lost near the epicenter and many people were inconvenienced because of the collapse of the infrastructure. On this same date, however, my new law partner, La'Chelle Woodert, and I had a new client meeting with the mother of John Greece. Mr. Greece's mother was hiring our law firm to represent him in a twelve-count sexual assault case. Upon further investigation, we realized the case was based mainly on DNA evidence. Because the use of DNA evidence was so new, this was one of the benchmark cases. Thus, we figured we would need a great deal of time before heading to trial.

In the interim, Austin and I gave birth to Brandon Jesse in June 1994. I was so happy to give him Papa Curry's name as his middle name.

After returning to work from maternity leave, I wanted to make sure La'Chelle and I were competent regarding DNA evidence, so I agreed to make myself knowledgeable in it. Meeting with DNA experts, visiting DNA labs, and learning the foundational as well as relevant evidence for Mr. Greece's case, was a huge learning curve for me.

During the pendency of the Greece case, I prosecuted and defended more cases in state and federal court. Then in May 1995, Austin and I got married.

The Greece trial started two years later. The biggest adjustment in addition to learning the DNA evidence was that Mr. Greece was incarcerated in Northern California. This meant the trial would take place there too, which required us to pack up and move up north for approximately two months for the trial. It was quite a feat especially with me having a toddler and husband at home.

Mr. Greece had been dubbed, "The Jogging Trail Rapist" by the local media because he allegedly attacked and raped three women on jogging trails. Mr. Greece was facing eighty years, if convicted on all counts. Originally the prosecution made an offer of approximately twenty-two years in exchange for a plea bargain, which they pulled off the table after it was accepted by Mr. Greece. Consequently, La'Chelle and I had a very difficult time even communicating with our client after the prosecution's snafu. However, as I observed interactions between my client and his mother, I began to resent the practice of criminal defense work all together. I realized Mr. Greece's mother spent all of her life savings ($250,000) with five attorneys over the years, including our representation.

I was at the end of completing my tasks for the trial, including finishing the cross examination of the DNA expert witnesses, when I received the heartfelt news that Granny, my mother who raised me since I was a teenager, passed away after suffering with Alzheimer's. It was on my ride home that I decided not to defend another criminal defendant. I was done and heartbroken because I realized I wasn't being fulfilled by my work anymore.

Shortly after celebrating Granny's home-going, I was hired to assist a family with estate planning. Upon completing the estate planning project, I had a conversation with my client. She inquired of her disability rights in a work-related matter. While we were talking, she referred to a police report that involved the reason for her disability. Upon reading the police report, I quickly realized the facts sounded familiar. It referred to my client who had been the victim of a robbery that took place around two years prior when she was managing a drug store. The report alleged that all three suspects were armed, and one particular suspect held a gun up to the victim's head and threatened to blow her head off if she didn't give him money. Then I saw the name Womack. I was speechless when I realized I was now viewing the same criminal matter Bobby Womack had shared with me in the halls of the juvenile court two years earlier. The combination of this situation coming full circle to me and seeing the emotional toll that my client, the victim, was enduring further cemented my decision to leave criminal defense work altogether.

CHAPTER 24

Chance To Win Over Darkness

Around my thirty-second birthday, I began attending a new ministry, Bread of Life Christian Center (BLCC), in Carson, California. It is a small, but love-filled ministry. I remember first being struck by the multicultural congregation. I thought it would be a perfect place to worship and teach Brandon to love all people. I had visited at least twice before meeting the pastor, Major Johnson, and his wife, Sylvia. Apparently, they were previously away on vacation. Upon meeting them, I was immediately struck by the fact that Major is African American, and Sylvia is Caucasian. As I sat and pondered this fact, I was reminded of my initial words to myself that this would be a perfect place to raise my son. But I hadn't considered my pastor's wife would be of another race. So, as I pondered further, I wondered why it even mattered. On that day, I prayed for God to remove any bigotry and prejudice from my mind and heart.

Brandon and I joined BLCC. I became an active member and learned more from Sylvia than any other woman in ministry. As a matter of fact, Sylvia made me look at myself in a whole new way. A couple of years into the ministry, Sylvia presented a women's bible study from T.D. Jakes' book entitled, "Woman, thou art loosed!" It was through the study of this book I realized I had harbored ill feelings for my sister, Dig, because I always felt like she put me in harm's way with my brother, Mutt. Also, I realized I had to forgive her. My forgiveness of Dig would allow me to receive forgiveness for what I did in putting my childhood friend, Rama, in harm's way with Mutt, too. I had totally forgotten about my despicable action toward Rama and certainly rationalized it because of my immaturity.

This study also freed me up to pray for Rama's wellbeing because of the pain I caused her. She has never been far from my thoughts and prayers.

In gaining my own freedom from the darkness of secrets and perversion, I was able to speak with Dig candidly about our past. Dig explained that although she too was a victim of sexual perversion and was unsure of boundaries with our brothers as a young girl, she revealed that she never told Mutt to come to me for sex. She was so hurt to learn what happened.

I also realized Dig did the best she could with the tools she had as a child. As the oldest daughter, she was the first target of Mom's boyfriends and Mom. She didn't know how to defend herself or us, but I remembered her trying. She didn't originally see Jesus as her way to freedom; instead she turned to drugs to sooth her pain. In using the drugs, she lost so much. In addition to problems with the criminal justice system, she also lost all five of her children to the foster care system. It was only after Dig came to the end of herself and found Jesus, she saw a better way. Dig re-gained her life as a daughter, sister, wife, mother and friend. She re-gained custody of her children, re-married, and birthed two additional children and graduated with her high school diploma at forty-eight years old. Also, Dig and Mom reconciled.

CHAPTER 25

Critical Chances

A couple of months later, I headed to Sacramento for a case with Brandon in tote because it was a perfect opportunity for him to spend time with my Sacramento family. Dad still lived there with my step-mother, Ms. Pearl. By now, Dad and Ms. Pearl were retired, and they had also raised Ms. Pearl's grandson and great granddaughter.

On the other side of town, Mom had decided to remain in Sacramento after recovering from the attack in Palo Alto. However, Mom and Dad could hardly be in the same room together for more than twenty minutes before all hell broke loose. The past always found a way to become the topic of the present. So, when I came to town, I made it my business to visit with them separately.

On this particular occasion, Brandon and I were visiting with Dad and Ms. Pearl, when she complained Dad hadn't been eating and he refused to go to the doctor. I did notice Dad had lost a lot of weight, so once we talked; he promised me he would go to the doctor the upcoming week. After we finished chatting, Dad drove me and Brandon to my niece, Shawnie's house, where Mom was visiting. As soon as Mom opened the door, after grabbing for Brandon, she commented on how frail Dad was looking. She said, "Ale, you're sick and you must go to the doctor right away!" After visiting, Dad agreed he would make it a priority and we left for the airport. Upon arriving at the airport late, Brandon and I missed our flight. This gave us the opportunity to spend the night and go to the doctor with Dad to attempt to get to the bottom of why he had lost so much weight. After visiting the doctor, Brandon and I made the afternoon flight home. About one week later, we received the news Dad was diagnosed with esophagus cancer. This was a hard pill to swallow, but this was just the beginning.

Apparently, while Dad's doctor was investigating the extent of the cancer, he stumbled upon a blood clot in Dad's leg which needed immediate attention. Dad set his surgery for the removal of the blood clot about two weeks later.

We were all prepared to rally around Dad in support of his surgery, but a couple of days before Dad's surgery, Mom had a massive stroke. Upon Mom's arrival to the hospital, the doctors discovered she had two aneurysms, one on each side of her brain. The doctors informed us they would have to operate immediately on one of the aneurysms to save her life, and another surgery would be necessary about one month later on the second one.

Hop, Mathis, and I traveled to Sacramento to be by both of our parent's bedsides along with Bull, Dig, and Bolo. Hootnanne was back in prison and had no idea of what was going on. Ms. Pearl handled all of the details and decisions for Dad. However, because Mom wasn't married, we, her children, were the decision makers, and we needed to be on one accord. Thank God Bull, Dig and Bolo had become Christians by this time and seemed to be working on becoming law abiding citizens. So, after hearing the pros and cons from the doctors, we all gathered in the doctor's office to discuss the options and pray. Each one of us spoke in an effort to ensure our perspectives were heard. It seemed great faith had infiltrated the room. After we all gave our thoughts, Bull weighed in. He stated, "Lord, if death is the deliverance, let it be." We all simultaneously moved from a place of humbled faithful warriors to crucifiers at the speed of light. I said, "What? What do you mean, if death is the deliverance? How can you have such doubt?" I was angry and confused all at the same time. I hastily encouraged Mathis to pray because I knew he had great faith and I didn't want Bull attempting to lead us with such little faith. So, after Mathis's prayer, we all proceeded to leave the room. We agreed Hop and I would share the news with Mom regarding her pending surgery.

Hop and I entered Mom's room. She appeared disoriented, but happy to see us, nevertheless. She questioned what was going on. It seemed some of her words were jumbled, but she clearly stated, "Don't let those doctor's touch me, I don't trust them!" We proceeded to try to calm her and lessen her confusion to the best of our ability.

The nurses arrived fairly quickly to take Mom into surgery. We were prepared for a four-hour surgery. After waiting six long, grueling hours, the doctor's emerged to tell us Mom survived the surgery and was resting in recovery. They anticipated we would be able to see her soon. But something went terribly wrong! The doctor returned to report Mom experienced complications during recovery and the metal clamp which was placed in her brain to stop the blood clot had come undone and slipped down in her brain. They rushed Mom back into surgery with little chance of survival. We continued to pray. This time after surgery, Mom was placed on life support and the doctors told us to expect the worse. We were counseled by the doctors to pull the plug and make plans for Mom's funeral.

At the same exact time, Dad was in another hospital across town. We split up so some of us could also go visit him. His surgery had gone well, but he too was still on life support. It was an unbelievable period of sadness and emotional anguish, but we just couldn't give up because we were people of faith.

Dad recovered and he was released to return home even though the cancer was still present, and he decided to refuse chemotherapy.

Meanwhile, we had an intense vigil at Mom's bedside. The doctors continued to ask us to consider pulling the plug and we continued to say, "No, we believe God. She will come out of this." After about two weeks, I returned home to Los Angeles to regroup. One night, I called the hospital to check on Mom. After I identified myself, I inquired as to whether Mom had gained conscious. A nurse began to share Mom's condition hadn't changed and wasn't expected to change because of the portion of the brain removed when the doctors performed the partial lobotomy and removed her learning box. I thought I wasn't hearing correctly as he must have been talking about the wrong patient because I knew nothing about a partial lobotomy or removal of her learning box. After I clarified with the nurse that he was actually talking about Mom, the phone went silent for a few seconds before the nurse said I would have to speak to Mom's doctor for a further explanation. I was shocked!

The very next day, I took the first flight I could get to Sacramento. Upon consulting with the doctors, it was explained that once Mom experienced complications and they returned her to the operating table, the small metal clamp which was used to block the blood clot had slipped down into her brain causing damage to specific areas of her brain. Consequently, when they took Mom back into surgery, they removed the damaged portions of her brain which ended up being her learning box. They further explained because her learning box was removed, they never expected her to understand or comprehend again!

We were so heartbroken. We didn't know what to do, but we knew Mom would not want to live in her present state. We asked about pulling the plug. And this time, we were told it was no longer an option because Mom's vital signs had normalized to the degree that death was no longer imminent. We now felt the doctors had betrayed us because they withheld important information from us which would've certainly made a difference in our decision the three times prior when they asked us about pulling the plug.

I needed a break from all the depths of the emotional toll this was taking on our family. I also knew I needed to somehow get to the prison to tell Hootnanne. So, the next day, I decided to travel to Vacaville State Prison to tell him myself. Upon my arrival, a lockdown was ensuing, which meant none of the prisoners would be receiving visitors until the security threat was brought under control. I ended up going to lunch with some of the other women visitors who were there to see their husbands and boyfriends. It was quite intriguing to have a bird's eye view into the life and mind of those women. They seemed to not be caught off guard by the lock down and to know all the ins and outs of the prison system. Each with their own story, some with relatively short terms of dealing with the chaos of prisons and others having made a life of being tied to someone incarcerated. After hearing all of their stories, they turned to me for mine. They were pretty surprised to hear I was an attorney just there to visit my brother. And after explaining our family trauma, by the looks of their faces, it seemed they didn't know whether to treat me like the outsider I was or feel sorry for me.

We returned to the prison four hours later. After being processed, I was escorted into the visiting room to see Hootnanne. He was very happy and surprised to see me. I decided I would keep the small talk to a minimum because I really didn't know how much time we had, and I wanted to make sure I told him what he needed to know about Mom and Dad's conditions to give him time to process before he returned to his cell.

Hootnanne was very shocked and saddened to hear of the condition of both of our parents, but he was fixated on Mom. He shared he had asked Jesus into his life and was living as a Christian in prison. He said he would pray for his release so he could care for Mom. At this time, our eyes embraced, and we cried. I remembered feeling jarred at the abrupt announcement, "Time's up!" Hootnanne quickly wiped his eyes and our visit was over.

After a couple of weeks, Mom's condition continued to stabilize. The doctors wanted to move her to another medical facility which would provide sub-acute care. Mom was moved and not long after her move   I received word Mom's condition had been upgraded. Apparently, she woke up from the coma-like state and looked around and said, "Hello." All of a sudden, Mom was seen as the miracle woman. She was able speak short sentences and seemed to understand. It was truly a miracle! We were so happy.

I went to visit Mom and I was so encouraged to see her progress. She talked to me. She understood me, but she had limited mobility of her limbs. Although I was still frustrated with the complications of her surgery, I was now so happy for the mix up with the doctors. I was happy they had actually withheld the information regarding the partial lobotomy because I realized had we known it, we would've pulled the plug and never saw any portion of Mom's recovery. But since we didn't, we were seeing God's power in a new, refreshing and miraculous way, so much so, that I was able to put my sibling's grumblings about filing a lawsuit against the doctors and hospital, to rest.

About two months after Mom's surgery, Hootnanne

was released from prison. Even though he put in for a release to be paroled to Sacramento because he wanted to be close to Mom, we received word he was being paroled to Los Angeles, since his last crime took place there.

It was certainly a bummer at first because I knew how much Hootnanne wanted to help with Mom's care. Shortly thereafter, however, an opportunity arose. Apparently, the hospital Mom was in was closing down and she would have to be moved to another hospital with the same level of care which also accepted Medi-Cal. After putting in a request for her to move to Los Angeles, we received word she was going to be transported to Gardena Memorial Hospital. It is located in a suburb in Los Angeles. Unfortunately, I believe the trip may have been too much for Mom because she never talked again after arriving there. We communicated with her by her using her eyes, smile and hands (thumbs up or down) to share how she was feeling.

Mom was so happy to see Hootnanne. She smiled from ear to ear. Hootnanne and I planned a schedule for visiting and caring for her. We agreed to alternate visiting days and to have at least one day per week to visit Mom together.

It seemed to take Mom a little more time to get use to me caring for her. Although she couldn't talk, I could feel heaviness when I visited her, especially by myself. I often kissed her, hugged her and whispered into her ear I loved her. I told her I forgave her for all the yucky stuff which happened. I also asked her to forgive me, if she felt I abandoned her. It took about six months for us to get comfortable with one another all over again, but we finally did. Hootnanne and I alternated days in caring for Mom, which was helpful considering I was balancing wifehood and motherhood. Brandon often accompanied me when I went to visit Mom and she enjoyed every minute of it. Things were going as well as could be expected with Mom's care and my home and work life balance until early 1997.

Around this time, profits in my law practice began to decline so La'Chelle and I parted ways. Austin and I decided I would close the law firm and find a government job. Unfortunately, this happened right after we started a home remodel. During this time in my life, I was struggling on many different levels. In addition to the family illnesses, I felt I failed my marriage as I hadn't found a full-time job soon after closing my practice. I was specifically challenged because I had people around me who understood how powerful my law license was, but they couldn't understand why I wasn't continuing to take cases while waiting for the new job. I knew, however, if I continued to accept cases and money from clients, I would never be able to pull away from private practice completely.

I had been introduced to a multilevel marketing company, Melaleuca. Initially, to purchase environmentally safe home products to help minimize

Courting with Chance

Brandon's eczema symptoms. But I also saw the business opportunity as well, and because I was in survival mode with my career, I chose to actively sell Melaleuca products. My people skills and great influence came in handy. I was able to capture the hearts, minds and pocketbooks of all who came to see me. I was good at what I did, but, not good enough. I was still earning money from some of my holdover cases in addition to Melaleuca, but eighty thousand dollars that year wasn't enough to keep up with the Joneses, which was the lifestyle we were caught up in at the time. Then, Austin had the nerve to tell me I was a disappointment.

Around this time, in September 1997, Dad and Ms. Pearl came to Los Angeles. Dad was really thin and appeared very weak from the cancer battle he was enduring. While in Los Angeles visiting Uncle Roy, Dad asked me to take him to visit with Mom. I obliged and took him to the hospital.

Upon Dad entering Mom's hospital room, she looked as if she saw a ghost. She was so surprised she gave her trademark smile from ear to ear. Dad seemed to be quite giddy too. They laughed, smiled and Dad talked for a long time, even reminiscing about the good old times. It seemed for a couple of minutes I was with both of my parents in a stress-free situation. They both were in good spirits. I had to actually shake myself out of a trans and realize we were in a hospital room with Mom incapacitated. Once I snapped out of it, I reminded Dad we had to leave because Ms. Pearl was waiting for him at Uncle Roy's. I gave Mom a kiss on her forehead and Dad kissed her on her cheek.

Unfortunately, this was the last time Mom and Dad would ever see each other. I visited Dad one more time in Sacramento after getting word death was imminent. Dad died on October 5th.

Approximately a month after burying Dad, one evening after work, Hootnanne came to visit me at home. He expressed he hadn't been feeling well. He had a hospital appointment for further testing to determine what was wrong with his stomach. He further commented, "If I die, I have seventy-five thousand dollars in life insurance for my three children: Lanna, Jona and Jason, Jr., and make sure I'm cremated." I thought he was talking out of his head, and I responded, "You should not be talking foolish like that because you're not about to die anytime soon."

Hootnanne had recently moved his partner, Rena, their daughter, Lanna and Lanna's cousin, Elana, from a third story apartment to a house. Soon after the move, Hootnanne got sick at work. At the time, he was working as an office manager for a construction company. They loved him and he really loved his job. Hootnanne assumed his sickness was due to over-exertion or possible food poisoning because he often ate from a food truck just outside the construction site at work.

Hootnanne was admitted into the hospital and six

days later he died. We were told he suffered a stroke in his bowels. He was taken to surgery, but his heart stopped while on the operating table. On November 13th, Hootnanne's spirit also took flight. I was devastated!

At the time of Hootnanne's death, my physical and spiritual vision was blurred. It seemed he was on the brink of getting himself together beyond a life of crime and drugs. My personal prayer and confession to him and for him was, "You shall live and not die to proclaim the glory of the Lord." I truly couldn't see how this could be accomplished with his death at thirty-four years old.

Dealing with the emotional toll of the deaths of my father and Hootnanne along with my career seemingly coming to a screeching halt, I was sinking emotionally. I went through the motions of life, but I confess, I was numb! I even lost my passion for practicing law.

Austin was also very grieved when Hootnanne died because he and Hootnanne had developed a brotherly bond. Between our combined grief and the thread of a relationship we were trying to hold on to, we were a mess.

CHAPTER 26

Chance To Overcome

After Hootnanne's passing, caring for Mom took on a whole new level as I was the only caretaker in Los Angeles. First of all, she had enough sense to realize Hootnanne was dead as soon as Bull, Dig, Hop, Bolo and I showed up to visit her on the evening of Hootnanne's funeral. She was already aware Hootnanne was in the hospital, as I had informed her earlier. Since he hadn't returned, and she was being visited by all of her other living children simultaneously, she figured it out. She just began to weep for a couple of weeks every time I saw her. Soon thereafter, I brought photo albums I inherited from Dad. I was thinking the pictures may trigger some fond memories. I was wrong on so many levels. She figured out the photo albums belonged to my Dad, and if I had them in my possession, he must have died. She began to weep even more for another couple of weeks.

Courting with Chance

Two months later, things seemed to have calmed down. Mom stabilized again and we were able to get even closer. I used the opportunity to test the limits. One day, I was reading one of Oprah's books about making better food choices. When Mom heard me say home fries, her favorite food, she gave a big sigh and smile and she actually said, "Um um." So, in addition to reading to Mom, I brought in a couple of her favorite foods on my next visit: greens and home fries. I took a little bit of the greens and home fries and put them in her tube. She loved it! It wasn't until later my nurse-sister-friend, Phyllis, who had provided physical therapy for Mom, told me never to do it again because the food could've been caught in her tube, and caused her death. I was horrified in hearing how something I was doing with such pure motives could've turned out so bad.

Meanwhile, at home tension was mounting. Austin asked me for a divorce. I was not ready to cross that painful bridge at that time. Still in denial, I thought I could save our marriage if I worked harder to find a better paying job.

The first job I applied for was with the Federal Public Defender's Office. A couple of days after receiving my application, they informed me by letter   I didn't have enough legal experience. I knew they were wrong because I had seven years of practice with several criminal and civil rights cases under my belt by that time. So, I picked up the phone and called a criminal defense attorney friend to ask him if he could find out the politics behind my rejection letter since he had previously worked there. He did, and I received another call from the Federal Public Defender's Office indicating I had received their rejection letter in error. They wanted to interview me. I interviewed with them and I made it to the next level of interviews, before they selected another candidate. I thought, "Oh well; I tried!"

Some months later, I interviewed with the Los Angeles County Public Defender's Office. Unfortunately, by this time my heart wasn't really in it, and I missed the oral interview cut off by a couple of points.

Then, one day, I received a call from Sheryl, my mentor from the City Attorney's Office. She informed me she had met with the Executive Director of the California State Bar and they were interested in possibly hiring me. I was thrilled and sent my resume right over as instructed by Sheryl. Much to my chagrin, that particular year, the entire state bar was defunded and closed down by former Governor Pete Wilson.

Austin and I decided to separate. Brandon and I moved out.

Yet, Austin still approached me about one more job possibility that would make him happy. He worked for a utilities company and had access to one of the company's senior executives. Austin asked the executive if he could help me with obtaining a position in the company. The only local position closely related to my qualifications required me to take a company test for upper management. I knew I didn't typically do well on standardized test, so I studied really hard for the management level test. Unfortunately, that job wasn't for me either, as I failed the test miserably.

Feeling tired and disgusted, I sought out professional counseling and pastoral help for myself because Austin wasn't interested in joining me. I also relied heavily on support from my sister-hood group, Sista Self. Since 1993, about fifteen girlfriends and I were a part of a support group with only two ground rules: First, we didn't want to formalize the group because we all had busy lives and careers. Second, we would not men- bash. We met the fourth Saturday of each month to encourage and uplift one another. These people resources were lifesavers in helping me cope during this difficult season.

One Saturday morning, I needed to clear my head. I took Brandon and we headed to the Mojave Desert to visit my sister, Hop, and her family. While there, I decided to go for a walk. I walked a little further than intended, and realized I was lost. It was in late summer and it felt like it was one hundred degrees outside. It was just me, God, the weeds and the devil. In my head, I clearly heard the devil say I was going to die out there and be found several days later. Then I prayed to God as I continued to walk. In my spirit, God told me my life had become much like my day's journey. I had lost my focus on God and was just going around the same territory like the children of Israel. I also discovered that I was mad at God for letting Hootnanne die so young. But on that day, I got clarity. I realized Hootnanne had lived a reckless, violent and pervasive life that caused pain to many. Thus, he was fortunate to have gotten a chance to turn his life around the last two years before he died. I was then thankful to see God's will done at the end of Hootnanne's life because at his funeral, thirty-four people confessed their faith in Jesus Christ - a person for every year of Hootnanne's life.

While still lost in the desert, I had another epiphany. Man's rejection is God's protection! I recognized living in a newly remodeled house with granite countertops, marble floors with floor warmers and high ceilings didn't make it a home. I realized coming from the dusty roads of Bakersfield, overcoming mental illness, violence and sexual perversion, I was a survivor. I had God, not Austin to lead me. I was strong, not weak. I kept walking totally oblivious to my surroundings. I repented and asked God to give me another chance. Just then, I looked up and realized I was no longer lost. I could see that I was just two blocks from Hop's house.

Shortly after my desert experience, I had a heart-to-heart discussion with Austin, and we agreed to start divorce proceedings.

CHAPTER 27

Chance For A New Beginning

Thereafter, I gained a new perspective. I was still seeking employment, but Brandon and I had been sustained by the grace of God through a couple of short-term client contracts. I also started dating again. I was introduced to a gentleman at BLCC, Dee. Dee was good looking and hardworking, but he was just a casual church goer. Also, around the same time, I received a call from Leslie, my attorney friend from Ernest & Sams. Leslie had terminated her partnership with Craig and went to work for the California Department of Justice, Office of the Attorney General (DOJ). Leslie worked there a couple of years before calling me to let me know they were hiring, and she thought I would work well for their agency. Upon obtaining the job announcement, I thought the position fit my abilities, interest and skills, but I was gun-shy from applying for jobs because of all the previous rejections. Dee called me out on my hesitation and encouraged me to apply, no matter what.

Within about six months into our relationship, I discovered Dee needed encouragement too because he revealed that he suffered from depression. I prayed and asked God to help me minister to him. However, as I prayed for Dee and studied about the battle front called depression, God also showed me how I too had been saved from the same pit after Hootnanne passed.

During this time, I joined the BLCC choir. One night at choir rehearsal we were informed one of our choir members passed away suddenly. After receiving the terrible news, I suggested we say a special prayer for our choir members because this news was too close to home. My choir director suggested I pray since I brought it up. I did pray and we completed choir rehearsal.

Later that night when I returned home, I realized I had forgotten to take my vitamins, so I just grabbed them off the bathroom counter and put them in my mouth. Without water in my mouth, right away my throat began to close up and I couldn't breathe. I was actually stunned because for a few seconds I felt like I was going to choke to death. I couldn't talk or yell for help, and in a panic, I couldn't even think to bend over the sink and try to get some water. Meanwhile, it was as if I was hearing a voice in my head saying, "You're going to die right here on this floor and your son is going to find you. Nobody can hear you." As soon as I heard that grim death announcement, I thought, "Jesus!" A pill flew out of my throat. Then I thought again, "Jesus," and another pill flew out. By the time the second pill flew out, I could at least breathe and open my mouth to scream, "Jesus!" The third pill flew out. I had been saved again by the name of Jesus.

Then on a Saturday afternoon in August, Brandon and I headed to Gardena Memorial to visit Mom. Mom was really excited to see us. She and Brandon played and laughed for the entire visit. After about an hour I gave Mom a kiss goodbye. Brandon didn't want to leave. He actually started to cry. After some consoling, he kissed Mom and we left.

That same evening, I received a call that Mom had sustained another major stroke. Upon arriving at the hospital, she was totally non-responsive. Thereafter, she just laid lifeless with machines keeping her body alive. It was so disturbing. About a month later, I called a meeting with Mom's doctor and my siblings to discuss taking Mom off of life support. After having a couple of discussions with Mom's doctor about removing Mom from life support, the doctor seemed to want to avoid the conversation. So, from August to December, Mom laid in the same lifeless state. In mid-December I spoke with all my siblings and with Mom's doctor again. All my siblings were in agreement that Mom should be taken off life support; however, in the meeting with Mom's doctor, he indicated that he wouldn't participate taking Mom off life support because of his religious beliefs. I respected his religious beliefs and requested another doctor be assigned to Mom.

Once another doctor was assigned to Mom, he indicated Mom could possibly live for minutes, hours, days, weeks, months or years after removal from life support, so we needed a plan. My siblings and I decided on a plan. If Mom survived after being removed from life support, she would be moved to a hospital in Antelope Valley so Hop could be closer to help with her care.

As if my emotions could not be spread any thinner, approximately two weeks later on December 25, 1999, my friend and mentor at the City Attorney's Office, Sheryl, died from ovarian cancer. I was devastated when I heard this news about Sheryl. But I was unable to dwell on it too long because my siblings and I were again charged with making a life or death decision on Mom's behalf.

Our prayer for Mom was different this time. With Bull, Dig, me and Mom's grandchildren at her side, on January 9, 2000, Mom was removed from life support. At first, we saw no immediate changes in her lifeless looking condition except all the machines were taken away. After about two hours, we took a walk across the street to decompress. We were gone from Mom about an hour. Upon our return, Mom appeared about the same, but her breaths were labored. It seemed as if Mom was waiting for us to return, because within twenty minutes, she took her last breath. Mom took flight after nearly four years in a sub-acute unit. It was heart-warming and heart-breaking at the same time.

I pulled Bull aside to apologize to him. His prayer for Mom in 1996 had finally come to fruition. As difficult as it was to admit it, death was now Mom's deliverance. My siblings and I who were there with Mom all cried and exhaled. I couldn't help but reflect on God's goodness in giving me an opportunity over the previous four years to show love to Mom. Notifying Hop of Mom's passing was the most difficult task because her hopes of having Mom moved close to her home to care for her were dashed; Hop was devastated.

Three days after Mom's death, I received a call from the DOJ for an interview. We buried Mom the following week. A couple of days later, I interviewed with the DOJ, turned thirty-five years old and obtained my divorce decree all in about two weeks. Whew!!!

Thank God I had also developed other relationships while at the City Attorney's Office as I couldn't have known Sheryl would pass away just weeks before I needed a reference for the DOJ job. Once I gained a reference from Assistant City Attorney, Bret Lobner, I received word DOJ's leadership had one hesitation in hiring me. They thought I would only remain with the DOJ for two years before leaving to become a judge. They didn't want to invest in training me for their position, for me only to leave shortly after. At that time, I had no plans of becoming a judge, but the fact that the DOJ made it an issue, made me pause and take notice. I had previously volunteered as a temporary judge to pass the time while I was seeking full-time employment. However, while volunteering, I gained insight into judging. I recognized that judging would give me the opportunity to make life-changing decisions for people just as a judge had done for me during my childhood. Once I reassured the DOJ that I wouldn't jump ship in the next two years, I was hired to start work as a Deputy Attorney General.

At work, I was assigned to the Health, Education and Welfare section under the leadership of Supervising Deputy Attorney General, John H. Sanders. John is a southern gentleman who became my mentor, big brother and even god-father figure. During my first year at the DOJ, Brandon lived with Austin during the week and with me on the weekends. This really gave me an opportunity to learn my new job. However, this arrangement with Austin came to an end when we had a disagreement regarding Brandon's schooling. Thankfully, my supervisor, John, was always accommodating for my needs as a single parent. Whether Brandon had a weekly doctor's appointment or an activity at school, John always reassured me that he understood that my child came first.

I was hired specifically as a member of the sexually

violent predator team because of my prior criminal defense and civil rights' prosecution background. While working at the DOJ, I obtained excellent training, discipline and confidence in my work product and ability to represent individuals and agencies, whether I was defending or prosecuting.

My work gave me the unique opportunity to work primarily in federal court in addition to arguing before the State Court of Appeals, California Supreme Court and the Ninth Circuit Court of Appeals. One of my fondest memories as a Deputy Attorney General was having my sister, Claudia, witness my oral argument before the California Supreme Court.

At home, Brandon kept me focused on being Mom. As he developed, I recognized his special needs unfolding. Nevertheless, because of his special gifts, he was always a trooper. I understood my role as a parent to love Brandon unconditionally. Also, my role as a Christian was to train him up for adulthood as a Christian and law-abiding citizen. In addition, I kept in mind he required additional assistance and patience because of his special needs.

Working late nights and traveling for work were a natural part of our reality. Despite daily ups and downs of being a single parent, Brandon had a pleasant disposition, love for school and he constantly strived to overcome his challenges. Brandon had a fully inclusive childhood and teenage life in our village community, yet he yearned for more of his father's attention. Thus, our village included both of my families (Ackerson's and Curry's), Brandon's paternal grandmother, Cecile, my best friends: Monique and Sharon (Brandon's godmothers); the support of our church, Sista Self, girlfriends and their spouses, neighbors, and wonderful colleagues. That same village community gave me the chance to fully participate in many career opportunities because I knew Brandon was safe. They were also the ones who came to our rescue whenever a crisis arose. And trust me, our village community helped us through more crisis than I can even attempt to explain in this book.

CHAPTER 28

Chance To See Full Circle Miracles

In 2003, Whittier law school invited a group of alumni to participate in an admission's ceremony at the Supreme Court. I understood the significance and decided to go as it was an answer to my prayer when I was there with Bernadette's family in 1988.

Before heading to Washington D.C., Brandon and I attended a Harvest Fest at BLCC. One of my DOJ law clerks, Cynthia, was also a member of my church. Cynthia was aware that I was leaving the next morning. She remarked candidly, "Make sure you say hello to Uncle Tom!" I was in total disbelief because I knew she was referring to Justice Thomas, but I quickly realized I needed to transform our conversation into a teachable moment. I responded, "That is not very nice to say about the highest-ranking person of color in public judicial office in our country. Actually, whether you like him or not isn't important because surely everything you know about him is from sound bites. What is important is for you to reverence his place in history." Cynthia was receptive to my comments.

On my way to Washington D.C., I stopped in Colorado to visit my brother, James and his wife, Ruth. While visiting, I came across a book in their guest room entitled, "Maximize the Moment" by Bishop T.D. Jakes. I picked up the book and couldn't put it down. I was so intrigued; I almost missed my connecting flight trying to finish the book before I left for the airport.

Upon arriving to the Supreme Court, I realized I was the only person of color out of the group of alumni. The importance of my participation became apparent for me after our group was placed in reverse alphabetical order to enter the courtroom, and as the last attorney to enter the courtroom, I was greeted by wide smiles, looks of surprise, and pride on the faces of several African American youngsters who were in the audience. After our group was seated, the Court Marshal called the courtroom to attention for the entrance of the nine Justices. I was aware, as the second African American appointed to the Supreme Court; Justice Thomas' appointment was controversial due to the Anita Hill allegations. His time on the bench hadn't quieted critics. But I was as glad to see him sitting on the high bench as the youngsters were to see me that day.

Courting with Chance

My name was called first. I stood tall and for a few seconds, which seemed like a lifetime, I stood alone and took it all in. Upon realizing I had come full circle in accomplishing one of my dreams, I began to look at each Justice one at a time. Although all of the Justices sat as if unmoved by the hoopla and exhilaration each of the admittees were experiencing, I could see from my peripheral vision Justice Thomas was looking at me. But, by the time I looked at him directly, I was shocked to see him look away. As I stood raising my right hand to take my oath, in my mind I thought, "Well, maybe he is what everybody says about him."

Then as I began to peruse back toward the other Justices, I saw someone peering over the bench from behind Justice Ginsburg smiling at me, so I did the courteous thing, I smiled back. It didn't appear that Justice Ginsburg realized the US Marshal (an African American woman) behind her was smiling at me, so Justice Ginsburg did what I did; she gave me a big smile. For a moment, I forgot I was in a courtroom surrounded by hundreds of people. I thought I had just experienced the ultimate one-on-one and I couldn't wait to share my experience with my childhood friend, Monique, my guest that day. I was so excited to share this experience with her. Monique had married her sailor boyfriend, Paul, and mothered my two godchildren.

After hearing oral arguments, our group exited the courtroom to report to the lower level of the court to take group pictures. We were greeted by a photographer who I engaged to negotiate extra pictures for our group. After taking pictures of our group, the photographer approached me to find out when Monique and I would be leaving because he wanted to take more pictures of us. After the group dispersed, we followed the photographer back into the building. After clearing security, we headed to the photographer's office to store our personal items before he began introducing us to courtroom staff.

As we walked through the hallway, the photographer pointed out Justice O'Connor's and Justice Breyer's chambers. I was in awe to discover we were touring the chambers of the Supreme Court. As we walked by each chamber, I took a peek in and typically saw a secretary sitting behind a desk. At some point we paused, and I realized we were standing near the red curtains in the rear of the courtroom, behind the Justice's bench. I felt chills just standing there. Then I inquired of the photographer as to which Justice was the most personable. He responded, "Believe it or not, Justice Thomas is the most personable." In disbelief because of how I viewed him earlier in the courtroom, I responded, "No way, he seems so aloof and impersonal!" Then I heard, "No, he's nothing like that. He is actually the one who is always willing to engage and embrace you." I was totally flabbergasted!

As we turned to continue walking, the photographer

pointed to our right and said, "Here is Justice Thomas' chambers." So, I looked inside and was startled to look right into the face of Justice Thomas! He appeared to be having a conversation with his secretary. I nervously said, "Good afternoon." Justice Thomas arose from his chair and approached the door. I held my hand out and said, "Good afternoon, Justice Thomas, I'm Attorney Karen Ackerson-Brazille, and it is an honor to meet you sir!" Then Monique held her hand out to say, "Good afternoon sir, I'm Dr. Monique Coleman, it is a pleasure to meet you." As I looked past Monique, I could see the photographer who appeared very nervous with sweat beaming down his face, obviously thinking he was in big trouble. He nervously chimed in, "Justice Thomas, Ms. Ackerson-Brazille was sworn in this morning!" Justice Thomas responded, "I am aware of that, ladies come with me." Justice Thomas motioned for me and Monique to follow him into his inner chamber to have a seat!

Upon entering his chambers, Justice Thomas entreated us for thirty minutes. First, complimenting me on taking the time to participate in such an important event as the admission ceremony. Then, he shared about himself and his family. He wanted to know all about us and just gave us some commonsense advice on how to not get caught in the net of politics. He believed politicians were either always campaigning or maintaining. He shared his candy drawer and laughs generously. He insisted Monique and I should be showcased on CSPAN because of our success stories in how I became an attorney and Monique, a forensic psychologist, given our childhoods.

While I sat taking it all in and looking around Justice Thomas' chambers, I couldn't help but admire the portrait of Abraham Lincoln, the bust of Frederick Douglass and the full wall of pictures of the shack where Justice Thomas was raised in Savannah, Georgia. Simultaneously, I realized I needed to find a way to maximize the moment, which was divinely given to me. So, I said a silent prayer. Then I opened my mouth and the words just flowed, "Justice Thomas, you have made much to do about staying out of politics. I have a desire to become a judge, and, as you know, that process is laden with politics. Furthermore, in California we just recalled the previous governor. How do you suggest I proceed in this political hot bed and be successful without getting bogged down in the politics?" Justice Thomas looked at me and said, "That is a great question and I have three suggestions for you: 1) Stick with the courage of your convictions. You can be persuaded otherwise, but don't jump back and forth between political parties; 2) do not hurt anyone. You can accomplish your goals without hurting others; and 3) I'll help you! People don't get because they don't ask. The first thing I will do is get you a mentor. Her name is Saundra Brown Armstrong and she is a Federal Judge in California. But, promise me one thing; promise me, no matter what you have to endure, that you will not let them steal your joy!" I reverently responded, "I promise!"

Since meeting with Justice Thomas, my life has not been the same. He truly inspired me. Justice Thomas impressed upon me that I could accomplish my goals no matter how difficult they were. Also, each time I wrote to him, he responded.

Furthermore, after meeting Justice Thomas, I returned to Los Angeles and telephoned Honorable Saundra Brown Armstrong just as he recommended. Her secretary answered and inquired as to my reason for the call. I informed her that Justice Clarence Thomas suggested I contact Judge Armstrong regarding possibly mentoring me. The secretary was very pleasant and helpful. She informed me Judge Armstrong was away on vacation, but she would inform her of my call upon her return. I was grateful and cautious when I thanked her and hung up the telephone. About an hour later, I received a telephone call from Judge Armstrong. She indicated she was vacationing in the Bahamas. But she would be returning home the next day and we could chat further. I was pleasantly surprised and stunned at the same time. We did speak again the following day. I shared portions of my story with Judge Armstrong in relation to how I met Justice Thomas and my desire in seeking a judgeship in the Los Angeles

Superior Court. Judge Armstrong shared her story of
how she knew Justice Thomas and gave me a little of
her history. She was so pleasant and engaging. We
scheduled to talk again and planned an in-person
meeting. We did. I traveled to Oakland to have a
shadow day. I was so excited to meet Judge
Armstrong and to be invited into her chambers.

Before meeting Justice Thomas and Judge
Armstrong, I had only previously been invited into a
judge's chambers for court cases with the exception
of Honorable Consuelo Marshall. Judge Marshall was
the first African American female Judge appointed to
the Federal District Court in the Central District. She
had presided over my first federal civil rights trial
many years before. After requesting her assistance, she
graciously invited me into her chambers to assist me
with my judicial application in the early stages. I am
forever grateful for having tea with Judge Marshall and
receiving her words of wisdom. Her help was invaluable.

In addition, Judge Armstrong was the first African
American female Federal District Court Judge appointed
in the Northern District. She taught me how to best use
my personality to embrace the new career I was seeking.
Specifically, she taught me to manage my family duties,
then my court duties, but to not stop there. She also
demonstrated how to be a servant to my community
once I took my robe off. It was so awesome to also

gain her wisdom and insight as my judicial application was moving through the process. I'll never forget the special note I received near the end of the judicial application process. Justice Thomas wrote: "What has happened with your nomination? We are on "pins and needles" here." His encouragement was unbelievably impactful.

CHAPTER 29

Chance To Obtain A Purple Heart

Leading up to my judicial appointment, my role as an aunt and mentor was challenged to the ultimate level. My nephew, Matthew Jr., left the Mojave Desert to join the U.S. Army at eighteen years old. Over the years, I continued to keep close contact with him. Shortly after entering the Army, he dropped Jr. and became known as Matthew, since his Dad had long passed away. Matthew married a fellow soldier, Vonnie, a Georgia native, who was stationed in Korea with him. After their tour of duty in Korea, they returned to the states, and later received orders for Germany in 2004. While they were living in Germany, I called Matthew and Vonnie to chat about the likelihood of them being sent to Iraq, given the United States was full speed ahead in taking down the Saddam Hussein Regime. Matthew shared he had been told originally, he and his family were actually going to be shipped back to the states because his mother-in-law, who was one of their dependents, was suffering from a severe diabetes which was too costly to be treated in Germany. Matthew's unit had already left for Iraq, therefore, he believed he and his family was state bound, but he was prepared either way.

A couple of weeks later, Matthew called to let me know plans had changed. Vonnie received an honorable discharge, so she would be returning to the states with their daughters and her Mom, if necessary. However, Matthew had in fact received orders to Iraq. I talked to him about how he felt. Matthew was very encouraging. He stated he believed he didn't choose to see this battle as just physical, but spiritual, too. He indicated just as Christ had to shed his blood for the remission of sins, Matthew felt blood shed was inevitable, even if it meant his blood being shed for the people of Iraq to obtain freedom. He wanted me to share with our family, if he died; he was ready and willing to go into battle and had no regrets. It was a difficult conversation yet relieving at the same time.

The following week, on Matthew's twenty-seventh birthday, he left me a detailed message on my telephone indicating he had been deployed. After hearing his message, I tried to resist the thought of him possibly being killed in battle at age twenty-seven. His father had died at twenty-seven years old.

A couple of days later, unbeknownst to Matthew,

his three-year old daughter, Shera, was in Germany with a Bible scripture on her heart. She ran through the house announcing to her mother, grandmother and her little sister, Shayla, "No weapon formed against me shall prosper!"

Back in the states, upon arriving and entering my office, I received a phone call from Vonnie, Matthew's wife. She was crying. She was trying to speak, but her voice was breaking up with emotion and I could hear her mother in the background saying, "hand me the phone." Vonnie said, "No, I can do this." About this time, my heart was racing on all cylinders. I said, "Vonnie, what is it?" She said, "I just received a call, Matthew's convoy was hit by a bomb. He's being transported to a hospital near Iraq, but they are not sure if he is going to make it because he sustained a brain injury. As calm as I could, I said, "Ok, niece, let's pray." I prayed for my nephew like never before, and for Vonnie and the girls before hanging up to try to figure out just what to do next.

After gathering my senses and emotions, I telephoned Hop's husband, Mathis, to inform him because he had been Dad to Matthew for many years. Mathis told me on his way to work earlier that morning, he was inspired to pray or Matthew and specifically for his brain. Wow!

I spoke with my supervisor, John, and made a couple of calls before leaving work. Upon leaving my office, I walked across the street to enter the parking garage elevator. Just as the elevator doors began to close, I heard an inner voice say, "Your family is prepared to receive this miracle." I took note, jumped in my car and headed home. Upon reaching home, my friend, Sharon, was there waiting. I jumped in her car and we headed for the airport post office so I could get my passport just in case I needed to travel overseas. While driving down Slauson Avenue in Los Angeles, I was surprised to see the marquee at the car wash, near La Brea. It read: "No weapon formed against you shall prosper. Isaiah 54:17." I took note. God was talking to me.

Upon arriving at the post office, I took my passport picture and got all my paperwork filled out before returning to Sharon's car. Once I arrived back to the car, my cellphone rang. It was my niece, Annie, Hop and Mathis's oldest daughter. Annie was calling to tell me Matthew was okay. In fact, he was on the telephone with Hop. I was in partial disbelief, given what I knew, but I also knew Annie wouldn't lie about something so serious. So, I just told her to tell Hop to call me when she was free. About an hour later, I spoke with Hop and found out more. I relayed what I knew to Vonnie in Germany and calmed her nerves. Vonnie relayed the scripture that Shera woke up with.

Then much later, we found out the entire miraculous story from Matthew himself, praise God!

Matthew's trip had originally been delayed twice. On his third trip to the base with orders for deployment, he was deployed. Upon arriving in Kuwait, Matthew was delayed further because his weapon had been lost in transit. Thus, his unit was delayed picking him up because they were all waiting for the arrival of his weapon. Matthew said one particular night while still in limbo, he and another soldier started to talk about the overall sentiments of the war. The other soldier was very discouraged and angry. Matthew used the opportunity to encourage the soldier about how God has a plan for each individual and for each soldier individually and corporately. Matthew told the soldier to not get caught up in the political hype, but rather see his life and mission as purposeful. After speaking with the soldier, the soldier indicated he felt so much better and he went to sleep. Within the hour, Matthew's weapon had been located and his unit arrived to pick him up. Matthew left and never saw that soldier again.

While traveling through the desert on the way into Iraq, Matthew heard a loud piercing noise and simultaneously realized his convoy had been hit by a bomb. Matthew could feel pressure in his head like his head wanted to explode after something pierced his skull. He said he remembered seeing the faces of his wife and children flash before his eyes, and he decided to have a talk with God. He said, "God, your reputation is on the line. If you let me die, it's your reputation that will suffer, not mine." Matthew still felt pain and pressure, but he also heard prayers and chaos all around him. He could hear his comrades trying to encourage him to stay with them; he could also hear them trying to make sure they could take cover. Then Matthew heard the noise of a helicopter. Within moments, he realized he was being moved, and then he could just hear prayers and see stars as the helicopter took off. He said it seemed to take forever before the helicopter landed. But, when it landed, he felt like he had died and entered military heaven. Matthew said he felt disoriented and all he could muster up was there were lots of officers waiting when the helicopter landed. Matthew could faintly see captain's bars, major's clovers, and colonel's birds. He said he couldn't figure out then why military officers were all saluting and pulling to take care of him. After getting Matthew off the helicopter, they took him directly into a room to prepare for surgery. Matthew heard the doctor tell him they had to operate immediately to save his life because he had shrapnel lodged through the center of his forehead projecting into his brain. Matthew was put to sleep and woke up a couple of hours later to someone asking him if he knew his name. Matthew replied, "Yes, I'm Matthew Ackerson." They asked, "Do you know your age?" Matthew replied again, "Yes, I'm twenty-seven years old. My birthday was just the other day." Then he was asked, "Do you know your phone number?" Matthew responded, "Yes, it's …" He gave the Germany digits, which were very long. The medical staff was amazed, yet happy. Matthew was called the miracle man. As a matter of fact, the two nurses who were placed on guard to observe Matthew couldn't help but ask him, "Who do you know? You aren't supposed to be alive." Matthew said he replied by giving them a smile and said, "I just know Jesus."

Once the medical staff realized Matthew was doing so well, they cleared him to call home to speak with his family in person. He called Hop and Mathis because the phones could only call state's side, not Germany. We were ecstatic to say the least. After about two weeks of recovery, Matthew returned home to Germany for continued medical treatment. He remained in the hospital for another month, with people coming by his room just to see the "miracle man."

Then a couple of days later, Vonnie and the girls were shopping at the Commissary. Vonnie happened to see one of the officers from Matthew's unit. The officer came up to Vonnie to tell her just how happy he was to hear of Matthew's miraculous story. He began to share the entire unit remaining in Germany was in shock and utter horror to hear Matthew's convoy had been hit. He said when he was told of Matthew's life-threatening injury, he wanted to crawl under his desk and cry. He realized if Matthew was hurt, and he carried the mantle of hope for all of them, they were all in trouble. He further stated if anyone could miraculously survive, he knew it was Matthew.

While they stood talking, a woman overheard the conversation and inquired. She said to Vonnie, "Are you the wife of the miracle soldier?" Vonnie beamed when she said, "Yes!" Vonnie recognized the woman was actually a General's wife. She went on to tell

Courting with Chance

Vonnie she had been told by her husband that he was out flying near the area where Matthew's convoy was hit when he heard an urgent call indicating two soldiers were down, one with a brain injury. The General instructed his pilot to circle the helicopter near the convoy site to see if they could find a place to land to lend a hand to the soldiers because the medical helicopter announced it was forty-five minutes away. Miraculously, there was a bridge within a couple of feet of the damaged convoy which allowed the General's helicopter to land for five minutes to rescue Matthew. The rescue mission was accomplished, which is why Matthew saw stars and heard prayers while he was on the helicopter. Matthew was seeing the General's stars and it was the General who prayed for Matthew.

After Matthew fully stabilized, he was released from the hospital. He met and thanked the General because Matthew recognized the "unusual" risk the General took in entering the war zone and rescuing him. Thereafter, Matthew's family prepared to return to the states.

Upon returning to Los Angeles, Matthew and his family surprised me with a very special visit at my church. One Sunday, while attending BLCC's service, Matthew and his family honored me by presenting and giving me his Purple Heart. I was humbled and honored to receive it as his first mentor.

CHAPTER 30

Chance To Make A List

In early 2007, Papa Curry passed away at eighty-six years old. I took some time off from work to reflect on how blessed I was to have had him as my father since I was fourteen years old. Also, I was grateful that Brandon had developed a close relationship with Papa in addition to his relationship with his paternal grandfather, Austin Brazille, Sr.

Once I returned to work, in my last big case assignment at DOJ, I was assigned to defend a federal civil rights case wherein the State was sued regarding the provision of wraparound services for children receiving foster care services. The case was entitled *Bonta v. Katie A.* On May 31, 2007, I traveled to Sacramento for one of my client meetings. Upon arriving, I went outside to catch a taxi which was my custom. I headed toward the first taxi in line which happened to be a blond

Courting with Chance

Caucasian woman wearing all pink. She introduced herself as Barbie. After she took and managed my bags, we headed out of the airport toward my hotel. She immediately started small talk. It wasn't long before we were talking about the similarities in our lives. She had also been a single mother with one son who didn't have a close relationship with his father.

I told Barbie I endeavored to only date men with long-term potential. Nevertheless, I didn't always get it right. Also, we commiserated on the fact that we both struggled with who would be a great mate for us and a great role model for our boys.

Barbie began to tell me her testimony of how she met her husband who is a great husband and stepfather to her son. She shared the Lord had led her to write a list of all the qualities she wanted in her husband, and to be sincere in looking at the top qualities before she invested in a dating relationship. Upon arriving to my hotel, Barbie encouraged me to pray and write my list before I headed to bed.

Praying and making a list of plans for my future wasn't new to me. As a matter of fact, most of my educational and personal accomplishments were met because of lists I made in the past. Typically, I prayed and put Bible scriptures and goals on 3x5 cards that aligned with my prayer requests and posted them in the entrance and exits of my home, or I made a list with approximate dates and posted it somewhere visible to me in my home. For some reason, I had gotten away from this simple affirming practice and Barbie was brought into my life to remind me of God's faithfulness in that regard. Once I arrived to my hotel, I did as Barbie suggested. The following is the list of qualities I wrote down in my calendar book:

1. African American

2. Mature

3. Christian (with own relationship with Jesus)

4. Confident in his own abilities

5. Married no more than two times

6. No teenage or younger son

7. Wants a son relationship

8. Not threatened by my success

9. Has own stability

10. Handy around the house

11. Loves good food. Can cook some

12. Loves people. Does not mind socializing

13. Likes to travel

14. Good money manager, but not stingy.

Courting with Chance

By this time, Dee and I concluded our on-again, off-again five-year relationship, so my conversation with Barbie was timely. Later that year, I started dating a southern gentleman named David, who was an active member of our new church, New Philadelphia AME (NuPhilly). Brandon and I had recently joined NuPhilly after leaving BLCC. David was a Christian man, very supportive of my career, and he worked hard to mentor Brandon.

CHAPTER 31

Chance To Pay It Forward

By mid-2007, I already took on much more responsibility in my assignment on the *Katie A.* case, however, I yearned to give back to my community as well. In that effort, I founded a free legal clinic, "Legal Eagles' Free Legal Clinic" at my church and recruited attorneys and law students who wanted to serve the community.

Then one afternoon, I was walking through the office headed to the mail room when I encountered a colleague, Felix Leatherwood. After exchanging pleasantries, Felix inquired if I had plans to attend the Los Angeles County Bar Annual Dinner scheduled for that night. Deputy District Attorney, Danette Meyers, was being installed as its president. It was historical because she was the first African American woman to take the helm of the organization in its one hundred and thirty-year history. Felix had tickets but he and his wife had a conflict, so he was giving them to me.

I decided to attend and invited Shelbi Walker, one of my volunteers from the free legal clinic. Shelbi had just graduated from a two and a half year accelerated law school program and I wanted to use this opportunity to congratulate and motivate her. After arriving at the event, I made sure to make rounds in the room to introduce Shelbi to as many attorneys as possible. Then I excused myself to head to the ladies' room. Upon my return, I spotted Shelbi across the room chatting with Honorable John Meigs. I was curious as to how Shelbi knew Judge Meigs. I appeared before him in my early years of private practice. I knew he was good friends with my colleague, Felix, but I didn't think I knew him well enough to have a personal conversation with him. So, I approached them and re-introduced myself to Judge Meigs, also mentioning we were at the event compliments of Felix's good will. Judge Meigs commented Felix had shared, during their morning walk; he had given his tickets to a colleague. Shelbi later informed me she knew Judge Meigs because he had volunteered on the Weingart YMCA Board of Directors when her father was the then-Executive Director.

Approximately a month later, one of my former DOJ law clerks, Antoinette Robinson, successfully passed the California Bar exam. She invited me to her swearing-in ceremony scheduled for Friday late afternoon in Judge Meigs' court. After arriving home that evening, I bemoaned the idea of having to go out again, but I needed to keep my promise and attend Antoinette's ceremony. I realized how special the occasion was and forced myself to drive to the event. I entered Judge Meigs' courtroom about two minutes after the scheduled time. Antoinette and her family were excitedly waiting. Judge Meigs announced, "Attorney Ackerson-Brazille, Antoinette wouldn't let me start without you, so thank you for braving Friday's traffic." I blushed because I was embarrassed, but glad I came despite how tired I was. Unbeknownst to me, Judge Meigs was on the secret judicial appointment's committee for Los Angeles County.

CHAPTER 32

Chance To Wrap Up Loose Ends

Near the end of my ten-year experience at the DOJ, I was privileged to have a courageous, passionate and vivacious legal secretary, Norma Herrera. Norma was a member of a local church which held an annual Christmas tea. Norma asked me if I would be the guest speaker for the 2008 Christmas tea. I laughed because I thought she was joking. I told her I would think about it. Inside I was humbled by her request, but also perplexed because I really had no idea why she would've made such a request.

Soon my possible fears were tempered when Norma told me another speaker had been selected, much to her chagrin. Norma remarked, "Don't worry, I gave them some choice words and told them you better be the speaker next year!" Now I was really shocked and embarrassed, but it also solidified why I had given

Norma the nickname, Lucy. Yes, Norma is full of excitement!

When the next Christmas rolled around, Norma revisited the topic and told me I was up, and I needed to be ready. I laughed it off because I was secretly hoping the tea committee would again select another speaker. Well, much to my dismay, they didn't. Norma returned a couple of days later with my marching orders which included the date, time and place. When I inquired of the theme, Norma simply said, "You come up with the theme. It's up to you." I thought, "Oh my God, what am I going to tell these people?"

As I prayed and thought about a message for the event, the only word that came to my spirit was the word "UGLY." For weeks I toiled over why I kept seeing and hearing this word. Then the Christmas tea theme came to me. UGLY was an acronym for "Unwrapping the Gift of Love in You." I finally realized it was time to share my life story publicly. Before this Christmas tea, I had only shared snippets of my life privately. I never thought the time would come to share the intimate details publicly. By this time, I knew I had been totally healed and delivered from the ugliness of my past and I had Jesus to thank.

After sharing my life story at the Christmas tea, I overheard a young lady at the event simply say, "No one can survive all that." I smiled and thought she was absolutely right because I couldn't have survived all that without Jesus.

Courting with Chance

Then a couple of days later, I met a close friend at Denny's restaurant for lunch after church. As we chatted, she disclosed she had endured molestation by one of her uncles as a child. She hadn't been able to move forward because of the pain. As we talked further, I encouraged her to consider the power of forgiveness she held. I told her to forgive her uncle so she could release herself to a newfound freedom. My girlfriend was adamant she righteously held on to the anger and bitterness. I knew I couldn't fault her for her feelings because they were valid considering she had been victimized, but I also knew the feeling of freedom from the release of anger and bitterness, too.

As we continued to talk, my cell phone rang. In answering it, my brother, Bull, was on the other line. He told me he was calling because he had been praying and realized he was in a lot of anguish because of some terrible things he did when we were children. He further said he was sorry for ever violating me. First of all, I was shocked he was calling, especially given the timing of the call. Secondly, I was shocked at his remorse and sincere heart. I responded that I appreciated his call. But I had no memory of him ever violating me. I suggested that he should call Dig and Hop because he probably owed them that apology. Finally, I did disclose I had been violated by Mutt. Bull then responded, "I'm so sorry, I was the oldest, and I am afraid I was responsible for teaching them all that ugliness." I was blown away! I thanked him and hung up the phone in total disbelief and relief all wrapped up in one. What I heard from my big brother at that moment was healing to me. It was also a total opportunity to witness the power of God. I was so grateful that I had started that conversation with my girlfriend.

Meanwhile at work, a federal special master was appointed on the *Katie A.* case. All parties were required to meet in Sacramento to work out details of a possible settlement. Some of our meetings yielded more than twenty participants because of the intense details involving my clients' social programs. Part of the integrity of the negotiations required all involved to be as transparent as possible to come to a resolution.

Before one of those meetings, I sat by a window and couldn't help but think about my childhood experiences in Sacramento. Coincidently, I had a view of one of the parking lots near the State Capitol where Hootnanne and I burglarized cars as mischievous youngsters. As fate would have it, during this case I received my judicial appointment in 2010.

I found great pleasure in notifying all of my family and friends who supported me over the years of the accomplishment of my judicial appointment. I was particularly excited to share the news with Judges Marshall and Armstrong and Justice Thomas.

Clearly, if I had my way, I thought I was ready for my judicial appointment around the time I first applied in mid-2003. However, God had a far different plan and timeline. God's plan was far more exciting than I could conjure up. God's plan included an Austrian body builder, Arnold Schwarzenegger, moving to America and landing in Hollywood to become an actor, then a politician, just in time for California to conduct its first recall for the Governor's office in the history of this state and recall its incumbent Democratic Governor Gray Davis, to elect a Republican Governor Arnold Schwarzenegger. Governor Schwarzenegger also appointed the first minority judicial appointment's secretary in the history of California's judiciary, Sharon Majors-Lewis, to recommend my appointment as Judge to the Los Angeles Superior Court.

Thereafter, one of my greatest memories of being appointed was to have both of my families attend my swearing-in dinner. Mathis and Hop (now pastors) blessed my robe. The next evening, Claudia and Brandon, enrobed me, while the Honorable Saundra Brown Armstrong swore me in as a Judge.

Two weeks later, I returned to the Supreme Court in my third biannual sponsorship of attorneys on March 31, 2010. I stood tall when Chief Justice Roberts pronounced, "The Court accepts the admission of the admittees sponsored by Judge Karen Ackerson-Brazille." While again quickly perusing the panel of nine Justices, this time Justice Thomas looked directly at me and nodded with a smile. Simultaneously, hearing the title Judge before my name was another one of my proudest moments.

The following day, on April 1, 2010, I returned home for my first day on the bench as a Judge in the Compton Courthouse to preside over criminal and drug court matters. Before leaving my chambers, I paused to think about my childhood in Compton. I thought, "God, you are amazing!"

CHAPTER 33

Chance To See Love Revealed

After obtaining my judgeship, I bought another home. I was still dating David who was living with me and Brandon. I noticed little frustrations were mounting between Brandon and David. Unfortunately, those frustrations grew, and immeasurable differences developed between David and me. Thus, we decided to part ways.

Sista Self was gathering for an outing downtown Los Angeles to see the Alvin Ailey Dance Troop in April 2011. Brandon and I headed to the event, but we first stopped at my sister-friend, Keri's house. She informed me she wasn't attending because her mother was sick, so she requested I take her two tickets and give them to Renata, another Sista-friend, who was bringing a guest. I looked at Keri's tickets and realized they were separate seats. I was thinking it probably wasn't going to be fun for Renata's guest to be separated from the group, so I decided to give her my tickets, not thinking Brandon should not have been separated from me either given his special needs.

Once Brandon and I arrived, I located Renata and gave her the tickets before Brandon, and I found our seats. I was sitting for about five minutes when someone approached me to inform me, I was sitting in their seat. Upon realizing it, I checked my ticket number and noticed my seat was directly in front of Brandon's. Once I got re-seated, I turned around to check on Brandon. As I looked back, I said, "Son, are you alright?" At the same time Brandon was answering, "Yes," I heard a man's voice to my left say, "Hey, Brandon!" And, Brandon said, "Hi Mr. Will." It caught me off guard, so I responded with a suspicious look, "How do you know my son?" The gentleman next to me said, "We attend the same church."

Our church, NuPhilly, endured a split in November 2010, with the founding pastor abruptly leaving to start a new church along with a majority of the members, including David. So, I assumed the gentleman sitting next to me must have been a part of the group that left, since I had never seen him before. I was wrong. He responded, he was presently a member and in fact hadn't joined until our new pastor arrived. He introduced himself as Will Gauff. Moments later, Elenore, one of the founders of Sista Self, arrived and

Courting with Chance

I was surprised to discover she knew Will. Elenore and her sister, Simona, grew up with him, but hadn't seen Will since childhood. We chatted a little more before the program began and during intermission. I did make a mental note of how well-spoken Will was. At the end of the night, we shook hands and vowed to look for each other in church.

The next day I was working in the children's church. At the end of service, I exited children's church to return the children to their parents in the sanctuary, and I saw Will. He was coming down from the choir stand. I made another mental note of how good looking he was. I stood at the door and watched him inch his way toward me. With his robe in hand, he approached me with a big smile and hug as he said, "Hey you." I responded, "So you do attend here, huh!?" From that day on we developed a new secret ritual. I exited the children's church room and stood at the door to deliver each child to their parent while simultaneously watching and waiting for Will to store his robe and come by to give me my smile and hug.

Apparently, we had never seen each other because I had elected to leave the sanctuary and teach children's church during the process of the church split. I was always neatly tucked away in children's church for the 10:00 am service and Will was attending the 7:30 am service except for the first Sunday, when we had a joint 9:00 am service. For the joint service, I was   still in children's church, but Will did get a chance to see Brandon in the sanctuary. Will said Brandon was always respectful and pleasant. Also, he had wondered if Brandon's parents attended the church since he had never seen them.

Near the end of August, Will and I began a telephonic friendship. It was interesting to find out Will had originally been invited to NuPhilly by a business colleague of his and a childhood friend of mine, Joslyn Wright. It was also refreshing to discover Joslyn hadn't told Will I am a Judge. He didn't come to know this fact until after we chatted on the phone for about three weeks.

In our telephone conversations, we also discovered we clearly had a unique bond considering Will checked all the boxes on the list of my fourteen qualities I prayed for in a mate. Also, we both were single parents of one son. Additionally, it was funny to discover Will spent a large portion of his teenage years down the street from the Curry's. It seemed we were destined to meet.

Then in November 2011, we had our first date. Will and I were engaged August 2012. We were married a year later before our families and closest friends. It was such an honor to have my father in the gospel, Major Johnson, along with Brandon, give me away to my soul mate, Will Gauff, Jr. After the ceremony, I'll never forget the heartfelt embrace of Will's adult son, Marshawno, when he said, "Welcome, Mom."

CHAPTER 34

Chance to Reflect

Having the opportunity to sit as a judge in a criminal and drug court assignment is a unique privilege for me given my life experiences. Often life-changing moments seem to happen totally unexpectedly. Once, I had an experience in my court which put my entire life in perspective for me.

I entered my courtroom and noticed a familiar face sitting in the back of the audience with a toddler in her arms. My bailiff, Deputy Roberson, informed me the woman was a defendant, Ms. Zettapart. She was back at court to request the termination of a criminal protective order since she had successfully completed her probation. Deputy Roberson further indicated the defendant wished to speak to me. In the interim, while I handled other matters, Ms. Zettapart stepped into the hallway because the baby was really excited.

As I thought back, I remembered the day I first met Ms. Zettapart. I entered my courtroom with my normal morning greeting, "Good morning staff, counsel and our guests." I called the case of *People v. Jane Doe Zettapart*. Once the attorneys made their appearances, Ms. Zettapart was identified in the custody box. I noticed a very petite woman, visibly pregnant and displaying erratic behavior. Ms. Zettapart was informed of her charges. She pled no contest and was placed on summary probation with the terms including jail time, counseling and drug testing, along with a criminal protective order.

Upon Ms. Zettapart's return to my court for proof of enrollment in her counseling programs, she had a positive drug test. I elected not to further incarcerate her, but to encourage her to consider her family, including her unborn child, who were all counting on her to become clean. Thereafter, Ms. Zettapart received all clean drug tests and glowing progress reports throughout that year.

Now she was back to have the restraining order lifted two years after her last progress report. After hearing all the other matters, Ms. Zettapart returned to my courtroom. Since the district attorney had no objection, I signed Ms. Zettapart's order as requested and asked, "How are you doing?" Ms. Zettapart answered excitedly, "Thank you for being my judge.

I want to let you know that my family prays for you daily." She further stated, "I absolutely hated you the first time I came to your courtroom because I was high on drugs, and I just wanted to return to the drugs. I couldn't understand how any woman would force me to stay away from my children for the period you ordered. But back then I had every intention of getting out of jail, leaving my good, hardworking husband and wonderful children, and heading straight to the drug house after stopping by the abortion clinic. I was stopped in my tracks because I was forced to remain in jail which gave me time to reflect. Plus, I was so grateful to receive counseling for all my issues and your words of encouragement on all of my subsequent court appearances made the difference."

I was humbled and frankly ready to leave the bench to enter my chambers to raise my hands and thank God for His goodness in sparing the life of a child. But, as Mrs. Zettapart was concluding her words of appreciation for me just doing my job, I interrupted to ask her the name of the excited bouncing baby boy in her arms. Ms. Zettapart paused and looked at me with a look of warmth that I will never forget. And she simply said, "I named him "Chance." "Chance, because you gave him a chance to live." I then dismounted my bench to give her and Chance a hug.

I returned to my chambers full of emotion. Reflecting on my life, I took off my robe and thanked God for giving me, a chance!